The Founding of the
Democratic Republic

The Founding of the
DEMOCRATIC
REPUBLIC

Martin Diamond

THOMSON
————※————™
WADSWORTH

Australia • Canada • Mexico • Singapore • Spain
United Kingdom • United States

Optically scanned and composed by Chas. P. Young Co.
Printing and binding by Quebecor World/Kingsport
Cover design by Mead Design

ISBN: 0-87581-271-6

Library of Congress Catalog Card Number: 80-84210

Wadsworth/Thomson Learning
10 Davis Drive
Belmont CA 94002-3098
USA

For information about our products, contact us:
Thomson Learning Academic Resource Center
1-800-423-0563
http://www.wadsworth.com

For permission to use material from this text, contact us by
Web: http://www.thomsonrights.com
Fax: 1-800-730-2215
Phone: 1-800-730-2214

Printed in the United States of America
25 24 23 22 21 20 19 18

Preface

These chapters are offered again to students of American government and political thought, with the conviction that no modern
account of the principles underlying our political institutions and
behavior approaches the clarity, thoughtfulness, and thoroughness
of these chapters—and with the conviction that such an account has
never been more essential. As a nation, we seem to be entering a
period of profound self-examination, during which we may come to
question the premise of the last decade that we have been a force for
evil in the world—exploiters of the weak abroad, oppressors of the
poor at home—just as, earlier, we had questioned and abandoned
the premise that we have been a force for good in the world—the
beacon of liberty abroad, the guarantor of rights for all at home.

When America asks itself a question like "what, as a nation, *do* we
stand for?", it has one very important advantage over other nations:
we have available to us a thorough, explicit account of what we were
intended by our Founding Fathers to stand for, in documents like
the Declaration of Independence, the Constitution, the records of
the Federal Convention of 1787, and *The Federalist* papers. The
most savage critics as well as the most ardent friends of the American constitutional order agree that those documents hold the key to
our national identity, since the Founders had been remarkably
successful at bringing to life a kind of political order that hitherto
they had only been able to admire in the writings of certain political
philosophers. Whether one considers that political order to be a
blessing or a curse to mankind, it cannot be understood (and
therefore, no national self-examination can be truly complete)
without a thorough study of the documents of our founding; and the
reader will find the chapters reprinted here to be an indispensable
aid to such a study.

These chapters, however, are more than a dispassionate, neutral inquiry into our founding principles—they are also a spirited argument. The title of the original textbook was not, say, "American Government," but *The Democratic Republic*—a forthright, and highly controversial, assertion that our government was designed by the Founders to insure that the will of the people, moderated and tamed by certain republican institutions, ultimately would prevail; the title flatly denies the argument of several generations of scholars that the Constitutional order was intended to protect the wealthy few by frustrating poor popular majorities. Martin Diamond is careful to warn the reader that nothing in these chapters should lead one "to be complacent about the profound problems that face the American republic;" nonetheless, he asks the reader to appreciate and enjoy with him "the subtlety, sense, and enduring utility of the fundamental framework of the American political order."

The great irony of Martin Diamond's celebration of the American political order is that, from 1937 to 1952, he had been an active member of the Socialist party, working to dismantle that very political order. Many young people of his day, and often the most intelligent and promising, had been drawn to socialism by its promises of—not just a better, but the best—tomorrow. According to socialism's utopian vision, there would be material abundance for all once reason had overcome nature; the human condition would be transformed so utterly that even physical appearances would be affected—all individuals, the socialist William Morris wrote, would grow to be "well-formed, straight-limbed, strongly knit, expressive of countenance—to be, in a word, beautiful."

The vast majority of Americans steadfastly refused to be seduced by the socialist vision, however, and as their most ardent appeals failed to stir even the most oppressed, Martin Diamond and his idealistic co-strugglers came to appreciate—the hard way—the versatility, subtlety, and strength of the American political order. The Socialist predicament is captured nicely in one of their sayings: "The masses are eager for Thomas and Krueger, but on election day, the votes are meager." (Norman Thomas was the long-time Socialist candidate for President of the United States, and a powerful influence in Martin Diamond's intellectual development.) The "votes were meager" for the Socialist party, Martin Diamond learned and later taught, because certain institutional structures like the Electoral College and the two party system steered American elections away from radical ideological politics, toward the politics of interest-group coalition and moderate, non-ideological platforms. And, the votes were meager, Martin Diamond subsequently would concede, because the masses simply were *not* eager for Thomas and Krueger. Indeed, American politics knew no "masses" as such—that is, groups of workers conscious of, and motivated politically by, a class interest radically distinct from the interests of the owning and ruling classes. Instead, American workers—and, for that matter, American employers—seemed to be fragmented into countless small economic interests, each struggling for narrow, limited material gains, and each seemingly content with the small creature comforts afforded by the commercial society. It must have been a bitter experience for the young socialists to see American workers content themselves with shorter hours and better working conditions, rather than reaching for the shimmering vision offered by socialism.

Idealism brutalized by reality often turns to black despair and pessimism, Martin Diamond later warned, and that danger must have faced him when he came to appreciate the futility of American socialism. And as he moved from the active world of politics to the passive world of scholarship, he would have found much food for bitterness toward and cynicism about the American regime. Ever since the scholarship of Progressive historians like J. Allen Smith and Charles Beard at the turn of the century, it had been accepted almost universally in the academy that the American political order had been founded by "tight-fisted conservatives," men of wealth determined to protect their holdings from restless masses of the poor. The seemingly irresistible assumption beneath this teaching was that all human thought and action are governed by class interest, or passion, or some other subterranean force; it follows from this that the Founders could not have acted otherwise than to have established a regime narrowly serving their self-interest. No wonder, then, that socialism had been doomed—the Founders had tilted the entire apparatus of government and society against it.

But Martin Diamond's move from politics to the academy had also been a move from the tutelage of Norman Thomas to that of Leo Strauss. Leo Strauss taught that reason was *not* inevitably in the service of economics or psychology, but may in fact be a force unto itself; this suggested to Martin Diamond the possibility that the Founders had *not* been motivated simply by class interest, but may in fact have been moved by thought and reflection—that is, reflection on the best possible constitution for the United States. Martin Diamond also learned from Leo Strauss the general shape of the ideas that must have governed the thought of the Founders; namely, that modern political constitutions are most securely grounded when they take comfortable self-preservation as their end, and when they employ the human passions, shaped and tamed by political institutions, as their means. After Machiavelli's assault on Christian rulers, Strauss taught, these would be the modest but attainable ends and base but undemanding means of modern regimes; political constitutions would never again be concerned with the admittedly more noble end of saving the soul by the unfortunately all-too-demanding means of suppressing the body.

That the American regime might be a modern, indeed, the modern regime—that concept suddenly, starkly illuminated the landscape of American politics for Martin Diamond, and became the fixed star of a dramatically new doctrine of the American regime. It now became possible to understand how the Founders could proudly claim to have established a democratic republic, even as they erected government structures that seemed to thwart democratic rule. As Martin Diamond will argue more fully in these chapters, the structures were not intended to frustrate popular majorities, but to channel and moderate them, and steer them toward sober judgments, by employing the quintessential modern means—the mild operation of political institutions on the human passions. Diamond will also argue in these chapters that Americans had come to prefer the humble comforts of bourgeois commercial society to the exalted vision of socialism and other idealistic doctrines, not because the people had been cleverly and undemocratically duped by the ruling class, but because the end of *all* modern regimes, based on the teachings of political philosophers like Locke and Montesquieu, is comfortable self-preservation through commerce.

But how could this regime of modest ends and mild means satisfy—much less find a vigorous advocate in—Martin Diamond, once a fervently idealistic Socialist? Perhaps the answer is that the intense pleasure he once found in imagining utopias, he now derived from the attempt to reason about the principles of the American regime, the modern project of which it was a reflection, and the great ancient alternative to modernity offered by Plato and Aristotle. For Diamond, the modest hope that reason could understand nature replaced the impossible dream that reason could conquer nature. And surely, the regime that not only offered solid comfort to the many, but also permitted him, and all thoughtful individuals, the freedom to pursue the intense pleasure of reflection was imminently worth defending.

Any defense of the American regime, Diamond knew, must begin by addressing the thoughtful and inquiring young people who were most likely to be repelled by the less noble aspects of the American regime, and to be attracted—just as he had been attracted—to the utopian vistas opened by socialism and other idealistic doctrines. No such defense had been written by the mid-60s, however, and the turbulence of that period, generated in large part precisely by young people seduced by various forms of utopianism, served to reaffirm the need. The true character of the American regime must be laid out in a textbook, Diamond knew, if frustrated youthful idealism were not to be followed by a bitter cynicism that the solidly entrenched and widely taught Beardian doctrine could only feed.

The result was, of course, *The Democratic Republic,* to which Diamond contributed the chapters on the Founding, the fundamental political principles, and the basic constitutional system. These chapters are even more important now, as we undertake our great national self-examination, because they offer a compelling alternative to the orthodox academic view that basically undemocratic American institutions have produced little but misery and oppression, here and abroad. If, in the course of that self-examination, we conclude that America is still the "last best hope of mankind," there can be no firmer foundation for that belief than a re-awakened appreciation, especially among the young, of the "subtlety, sense, and enduring utility of the fundamental framework of the American political order."

William A. Schambra
American Enterprise Institute
Washington D.C. 1980

Contents

Chapter 1

INTRODUCTION

We hold these truths to be self-evident, that all men are created equal, that they are endowed by their Creator with certain unalienable Rights, that among these are Life, Liberty, and the pursuit of Happiness.—That to secure these rights, Governments are instituted among Men, deriving their just powers from the consent of the governed. . . .

—THE DECLARATION OF INDEPENDENCE[1]

To secure the public good and private rights against the danger of [an overbearing majority], and at the same time to preserve the spirit and form of popular government is then the great object to which our inquiries are directed.

—THE FEDERALIST[2]

The Declaration of Independence did more than declare the thirteen colonies independent of Great Britain. Indeed that was done on July 2 by a simple resolution of the Continental Congress. But we rightly celebrate July 4 and not July 2 as our national holiday because, while actions sometimes speak louder than words, words usually give to actions their political meaning and consequence. The continuing importance of the Declaration lies in the principles by which it justified independence. That is, the Declaration grounded separation from Britain upon principles of government held to be valid for all men at all times. These principles became the credo of the American political order—but only after a remarkable transformation that culminated in the Constitution.

We must thus see the Declaration in its relationship to the Constitution. Together they shape the nature of the American political order. In turn, one's understanding of the relationship between these two fundamental documents shapes one's understanding of the modern American political system. Accordingly, the basic approach and themes of this book can be unfolded by tracing the theoretical transformation of the Declaration by the Constitution.

The Declaration as the National 'I Believe'

It is commonplace to say that the Declaration of Independence is the national political credo. Nothing in that strikes the American ear as odd. It is so commonplace that we do not see how unique and significant it is to have a national credo. Consider the root of the word: *Credo* from the Latin for I believe. The principles of the Declaration are the national 'I believe'; to be an American, it is assumed, is to believe in those principles.

The creedal character imparted to American life by the Declaration is revealed in several uniquely American terms and usages. Consider the term Americanism; no other country has an expression quite like it. How can America be an ism?

> When we examine the meaning of Americanism, we discover that Americanism is to the American not a tradition or a territory, not what France is to a Frenchman or England to an Englishman, but a doctrine—what socialism is to a socialist. . . . a highly attenuated, conceptualized . . . assent to a handful of final notions—democracy, liberty, opportunity.[3]

The term Americanism thus reflects a unique phenomenon. Other countries have no single political doctrine, adherence to which is a kind of national obligation or heritage. Frenchmen, for example, are no less French in being clericalists, or monarchists, or republicans, or Gaullists, or communists, or fascists. But to be an American has meant somehow to accept the fundamental credo; deviation from it causes one to be regarded as un-American (another expression which has no analogue elsewhere).[4] The term Americanism expresses the conviction that American life is uniquely founded on a set of political principles, superior to those of the rival modern ideologies. And this American ism consists in certain "final notions" regarding the relationship of "democracy, liberty, opportunity."

The term Americanization—widely used during the mass immigration period—points similarly to the creedal framework of American politics. Americanization meant more than the mere adoption by immigrants of American clothes, speech, and social habits; to become Americanized meant to acquire the political ideas peculiarly appropriate to America. Other countries that have had substantial immigration did not develop a concept or term like Americanization. The French did not Gallicize immigrant Algerians, nor do the English Anglicize their Commonwealth immigrants in the political sense of Americanization. French and English immigrants had, so to speak, to become acculturated; in America, immigrants had to be politicized.

Consider similarly the Pledge of Allegiance. National loyalty or allegiance means, typically, unqualified fidelity to a fatherland. Americans pledge their allegiance not to a fatherland but to a republic, a distinctive form of government; and their pledge is not unconditional, but rather is hedged round with a remarkable set of conditions. Americans promise to be loyal only to the republic for which the flag stands. As it were, the deal is off if America abandons the republican form. Indeed loyalty is promised only to an indivisible republic, a post-Civil War slap at southern secessionism. Further, allegiance is pledged only so long as the republic, under God, seeks to deliver liberty and jusice for all. In short, patriotism—from the Greek for fathers, meaning love of one's forebears and unqualified loyalty to them—in the American case means love of the Founding Fathers and loyalty to their political principles.

American life thus regards itself as founded on a set of political principles—one can almost say, a set of doctrines. Rare is the country which to the same degree lives upon its past so explicitly, and with as much agreement on principles descended from that past.[5] But what precisely are those principles?

The Declaration: A Democratic Document?

Democracy and Liberty: That fairly well sums up the popular—and, for that matter, much scholarly—opinion of what the Declaration represents. The Declaration is thought to proclaim a democratic regime in which government functions by consent of the governed in such a way as to secure a free society. But in fact the Declaration does not do that at all. The popular understanding has read democracy into the Declaration; we have come to see the Declaration through the transforming lens of two centuries of successful democratic government.

Let us look at the Declaration closely to see what it actually says. The Declaration holds four truths to be "self evident"—that all men are created equal, that they are endowed by their Creator with certain unalienable rights, that governments, whose proper end is to secure these rights, may only be instituted by the consent of those to be governed, and that, when government becomes destructive of these rights, the people have the further right to alter or abolish and reinstitute their government.

Of these four truths, the middle two (when transformed) form the center of the American credo. The last is, strictly speaking, not a governing principle, but rather is the right of revolution. The first—that all men are created equal—is the primal truth, the one from which the other three are derived. Following from the primal truth of human equality, the two central ones concern the end of government and its institution. The end of government is to secure to equal men the rights to life, liberty, and the pursuit of happiness; legitimate governments may be instituted only by the consent of those to be governed.

Unalienable rights and consent of the governed, these are indeed the central principles of the American credo. But by consent of the governed the Declaration did not mean what it has come to mean in the credo. We have transformed the Declaration by reading consent of the governed as rule by majorities, that is, democratic government. But the Declaration does not say that consent is the means by which government is to be *operated;* rather, consent is necessary only to *institute* the government, that is, to establish it. The people need not, however, establish a government which operates by means of their consent. Rather, they may organize it on "such principles" as they choose, and they may choose "any form of government" they deem appropriate to secure their rights. That is, the Declaration was not urging a particular form of government, but rather was following John Locke's social contract theory which taught the right of the people to establish any form of government they chose.

And by *any* form of government the Declaration includes democratic or aristocratic or monarchic government. That is why the Declaration has to accuse the British king of a "long train of abuses." Tom Paine, for example, believed George III unfit to rule simply because he was a *king*, and kingly rule was illegitimate. On the contrary, the Declaration holds George III "unfit to be the ruler of a free people" not because he was a king, but because he was a *tyrannical* king. Rather than securing to the Americans their rights, his rule had become "destructive of these ends"; therefore, and only therefore, the colonists were entitled to rebel.

Thus the Declaration, although it is now seen as the very embodiment of the democratic spirit, was in fact neutral with regard to the democratic form of government. (As we shall see, it was the Constitution that embodied the democratic principle, and thus transformed our understanding of the Declaration.) Although the new nation "was conceived in liberty, and dedicated to the proposition that all men are created equal," the Declaration only required that government be of the people and for the people, but not *by* the people. Ironically, then, the Declaration offers no guidance for constituting or preserving democratic government. Accordingly, Thomas Jefferson, the chief author of the Declaration, could agree when James Madison made precisely this point to him.

The true doctrines of liberty, as exemplified in our Political System, should be inculcated on those who are to sustain and may administer it. . . . [But it is not] easy to find standard books that will be both guides and guards for that purpose. Sydney and Locke are admirably calculated to impress on young minds the right of nations to establish their own governments, and to inspire a love of free ones, but afford no aid in guarding our Republican charters against constructive violations. The Declaration of Independence, tho rich in fundamental principles . . . *falls really under a like observation.* (emphasis added)[6]

In short, although the Declaration taught men their right to "establish their own governments" and inspired "a love of free ones," it did not prescribe the democratic form of government. As to that, strictly read, the Declaration says no more than this: If you choose the democratic form or mode of government, it should be constructed and operated so as to be a *free* government. But how to do that? The Declaration is silent. Accordingly, Madison stressed and Jefferson agreed that the Declaration afforded "no aid in guarding our Republican charters."[7]

The Declaration: Credo and Problem

Even when read as it has come to be understood—as the credo of a free democratic system—the Declaration affords little aid in constructing and operating such a system. Even if we assume "consent of the governed" means government by consenting majorities, and that "unalienable rights" means that democratic government may do only certain things and those only in certain ways, we notice that the Declaration poses a problem which it does not itself solve. Namely, the Declaration's two principles thus construed— democratic majority rule and liberty—are not automatically harmonious. Indeed they can be sharply opposed. Witness their problematical relationship, for example, in Jefferson's First Inaugural Address. He spoke of the "sacred principle, that though the will of the majority is in all cases to prevail, that will to be rightful must be reasonable." Consent of the governed has become majority rule; and by reasonable Jefferson refers to the realm of unalienable rights. Jefferson rightly implies that the two principles may conflict in practice. What if the majority consents to unreasonable or tyrannical things, or indeed demands them? What if men, on the majority rule principle, vote away the liberty (of minorities, or even their own) which is the other principle of the Declaration. Or what if, under the cloak of liberty, a conspiratorial or obstructive minority undermines the very possibility of majority? Reconciling this potential conflict of democracy and liberty has always been a prime task of the American political order.

And what about the *competence* of government? How can a government, operating by majority rule and aiming at the preservation of liberty, be rendered adequate to the sheer task of governing? On that question, which has always troubled students of American government, now perhaps more than ever, the Declaration is of course silent. Whether it is strictly understood as neutral respecting democracy, or as it came to be democratically understood, the Declaration does not offer solutions to the problem of reconciling democracy, liberty, and the necessities of competent government.

Yet, after all, that was not its job. It sought to rally the colonists—and indeed the world—to the American struggle for independence by declaring the principles which animated the struggle. And that was enough. But the Declaration's unfinished business—reconciling the competing demands of democracy, liberty, and competent government—was precisely the task to which the Constitution was addressed.

THE DEMOCRATIC REPUBLIC

The Constitution transformed and completed the work of the Declaration. The Declaration could not become the American 'I believe' until it came to be read as the inspiriting credo of a democratic political order, namely, the free and competent frame of government established by the Constitution.[8]

Few countries have a national political creed. Fewer have a formal constitution vitally related to that creed. It is no accident, therefore, that much American political debate and scholarship has focussed on the relationship between the Declaration and the Constitution; or to state the issue more precisely, on the relationship between democracy and the restraining tendencies of the Constitution. This relationship is at the center of the American political existence. Everything depends upon its proper understanding. As could be expected, there are conflicting views.

Most scholars during this century have not viewed the Constitution as a faithful attempt to solve the Declaration's problem. Rather, they believe that the Framers were so concerned with liberty—or, more bluntly, with the privileges of the wealthy—that they deliberately retreated from the democratic spirit of the Declaration. Or they regard the Constitution as embodying a pessimistic and obsolete eighteenth-century view of man as naturally depraved and prone to tyranny, and thus in need of a confining and limiting government. In either case, they see the Constitution as establishing governmental structures and processes deliberately calculated to frustrate the will of the majority.

This influential view of the 'undemocratic Constitution' may be seen in still another way. Modern conservatives and liberals alike often pit the informal *democratic* elements of the American political order against the formal constitutional *republican* elements. The democratic elements they both portray as resting upon clear-cut appeals to popular majorities, strong national government, and executive leadership to achieve "the general welfare." The republican elements they portray as resting upon deadlocking checks and balances, federalism, and limited government to secure "the blessings of liberty," especially for propertied minorities. Both conservatives and liberals thus portray a divided political system at war with itself, with the democratic forces gradually overcoming the stubborn republican restraints.[9]

This book, as its title indicates, rejects the view of the undemocratic Constitution, and consequently offers a different interpretation of the American political order, both as it was designed and as it functions today. We argue that the Constitution is not undemocratic and was not a retreat from democracy. Rather, it is a thoroughgoing effort to *constitute democracy*. We view the American system as seeking to reconcile the advantages of democracy with the sobering qualities of republicanism. Such reconciliation is the central fact. American political history is the experience of the successes and failures of that reconciliation. Similarly, the principles and processes of modern American government and politics are best understood when the system is grasped in its essential quality, namely, as a democratic republic.

Or to state it another way: we argue that the American system still rests today upon a theory which informed its construction, a theory which seeks to render a democratic regime compatible with the protection of liberty and the requisites of competent government. To understand that theory and thus the principles which form the character of the American political order, we must begin by understanding how the men who designed that order saw the problem of democracy.

Decent Even Though Democratic?

The most difficult thing to grasp is the Framers' cool acceptance of the democratic form of government. The modern tendency is to assume that if a system is not democratic it cannot be decent; the Framers, on the contrary, believed that if a system were democratic, it would be extraordinarily hard to make it decent. Jacobin enthusiasts cannot believe that men who so coolly discussed democracy's intrinsic defects could in fact have opted for democracy. Such enthusiasts see no intrinsic difficulties in democracy; in contrast with the Framers, they subscribe to the comforting doctrine that 'whatever is wrong with democracy can be cured by more democracy.' On the other hand, conservative anti-democrats cannot believe that men who so sensibly saw democracy's defects and dangers could possibly have accepted democracy. But they did, and both the coolness and the acceptance are the key to understanding the leading Framers. Consider James Madison:

> To secure the public good and private rights against the danger of [an overbearing majority], and at the same time to preserve the spirit and the form of popular government is then the great object to which our inquiries are directed. Let me add that it is the great desideratum by which alone this form of government can be rescued from the opprobrium under which it has so long labored and be recommended to the esteem and adoption of mankind.[10]

No intelligent man, Madison is saying, had hitherto been able to espouse popular (i.e., democratic) government, because it had been incompatible with the public good and private rights. But now—and notice the remarkable claim—for the first time we have the knowledge and opportunity to make democracy decent. The Constitution establishes a government, faithful to the spirit and form of democracy, which nonetheless guards against its dangerous propensities.

As the dedication of this book to Madison indicates, we follow his understanding of the fundamental thrust of the American political system. Accordingly, throughout the book we study how the American system deals or fails to deal democratically with the problems of Liberty and competent government. It suffices here to summarize the Framers' reasoning regarding the defective tendencies of democracy, and how they thought their system would cope with them.

Stability and Energy Versus Freedom and Democracy? The problem of democracy was its dangerous propensities to folly, feebleness, and tyranny. Notice: not just tyranny, but folly and feebleness as well; not just tyrannical majorities, but ignorant and erratic majorities as well. Nothing could be more misleading than the familiar simplistic view that the Framers were solely concerned to protect liberty and hence were hostile to strong government. In the first place, the leading Framers knew that liberty could only be secured under a strong and stable government; and further they knew that strong government is necessary to cope with the problems societies face. Thus they had to solve the problem of majority rule on two fronts; their government had to generate human conduct that would lessen the likelihood of either democratic tyranny or democratic ineptitude.

In contrast to monarchy and aristocracy (or as we might now say, dictatorship or totalitarianism), democracy had never been able to achieve strong and stable government. The difficult task, therefore, was to combine "the requisite stability and energy in government, with the inviolable attention due to liberty, and to the republican form."[11] But stability and energy require institutions and processes that seem to go against the grain of liberty and popular government. A free democracy requires that power be dispersed in many hands and that public officers be subject to frequent change according to the will of the majority. But stability, on the contrary, requires that the same men hold power long enough to persist in a consistent set of policies; and energetic government requires execution, not by a multiplicity of officers, but by a single hand. Thus, concentration and duration of power are, at the same time, indispensable to competent government, and inimical to the requisites of democratic freedom.

As to the more familiar side of the Framers' thought—their concern with liberty—we may summarize their reasoning with a quotation from their contemporary, the English philosopher and statesman, Edmund Burke:

> In a democracy the majority of the citizens is capable of exercizing the most cruel oppressions upon the minority, whenever strong divisions prevail in that kind of polity, as often they must, and that oppression of the minority will extend to far greater numbers and will be carried on with much greater fury, than can almost ever be apprehended from the dominion of a single sceptre. . . . Under a cruel prince they have the balmy compassion of mankind to assuage the smart of their wounds and they have the plaudits of the people to animate their generous constancy under their sufferings: but those who are subjected to wrong under multitudes are deprived of all external consolation; they seem deserted by mankind, overpowered by a conspiracy of their whole species.[12]

In short, majority rule is inescapable in the democratic form of government and, at the same time, inherently capable of converting that government into an intolerable despotism.

The Framers thus had to create a system of institutions and procedures that would satisfy their complex aim: powerful and yet free government resting upon majority rule. They could not simply weaken or limit government to secure liberty, nor could they simply render it so powerful as to destroy liberty, nor could they evade the final authority of the majority. They built their regime upon a theory that taught a way to tame and temper democracy. Whether that regime is adequate today may well be challenged. But those who challenge the regime are well advised to grasp first the theory upon which the regime rests.

. . . . .

BIBLIOGRAPHICAL NOTE

Useful introductions to the origin of the American republic are: Louis Hartz, *The Liberal Tradition in America* (1953); Edmund S. Morgan, *The Birth of the Republic* (1956); Clinton Rossiter, *Seedtime of the Republic* (1952). Seymour Martin Lipset, *The First New Nation* (1963) treats American political history in the context of contemporary studies of the founding of new nations in Asia and in Africa.

Carl Becker, *The Declaration of Independence* (1922) presents the background of the document. Abraham Lincoln's "Springfield Address of 1857" analyzes the Declaration. Martin Diamond, "The Revolution of Sober Expectations" in *America's Continuing Revolution* (1976) examines the Revolution and analyzes the Declaration.

Martin Diamond, "The Declaration and the Constitution: Liberty, Democracy, and the Founders," in Nathan Glazer and Irving Kristol, eds., *The American Commonwealth—1976* (1976) and "The American Idea of Equality," in *Review of Politics* (1976) explore the relationship between liberty and equality.

Charles H. McIlwain, *The American Revolution* (1923) analyzes the colonial legal argument. J. Franklin Jameson, *The American Revolution Considered as a Social Movement* (1926) emphasizes democratic change. Robert Brown, *Middle-class Democracy and the Revolution in Massachusetts* (1955) emphasizes the degree of democracy prior to the Revolution. Charles S. Sydnor, *Gentlemen Freeholders* (1952) emphasizes aristocratic aspects of Virginia politics of the period. Robert R. Palmer, *The Age of the Democratic Revolution* (1959) places the American Revolution within the context of contemporary western European democratic developments.

Edmund C. Burnett, *The Continental Congress* (1941) and Allan Nevins, *The American States during and after the Revolution* (1924) are standard works on their respective subjects.

Andrew C. McLaughlin, *The Confederation and the Constitution* (1940), John Fiske, *The Critical Period in American History* (1883), which sharply criticizes the Articles, and Merrill Jensen, *The Articles of Confederation* (1940), which defends them, are three important works on this disputed subject.

The Reconstruction of American History (1962), John Higham, ed., contains several essays on conflicting points of view regarding the same matters treated in this chapter. A recently emerging point of view is that of the so-called 'New Left' historians; two representative works are Staughton Lynd, *Class Conflict, Slavery and the United States Constitution* (1967), and Barton J. Bernstein, ed., *Toward a New Past: Dissenting Essays in American History* (1968).

The People Shall Judge (1949), The Staff, Social Sciences I, The College of the University of Chicago, eds., is an excellent collection of original documents relating to American origins and early political problems.

NOTES

[1] The full text of the Declaration is reproduced in the Appendix, as is the text of the Constitution.

[2] *Federalist* 10. This and all subsequent references are to *The Federalist*, with an introduction by Clinton Rossiter (New York: New American Library Mentor Books, 1961). The student will find valuable the "Index of Ideas" prepared by Rossiter.

[3] Leon Samson, *Toward a United Front: A Philosophy for American Workers* (New York: Farrar & Rinehart, Inc., 1933), p. 16.

[4] In England or France, something alien may be criticized as un-English or un-French; but this has a cultural more than a political meaning. Thus neither England nor France could have anything like a House Committee on Un-American Activities.

[5] Ironically, the Soviet Union and some other communist countries are the closest analogue of America in this respect. Only Russia has made a part of its national name into an ism—Sovietism—and tries to make its national identity coincident with a specific set of political principles; thus they tend to treat Marx, Engels, and Lenin as their Founding Fathers, and certain venerated texts as the basis of their regime.

[6] James Madison to Thomas Jefferson regarding a program of readings at the University of Virginia, February 8, 1825 (*Madison Papers,* Vol. 74, Library of Congress, Series 2, p. 36). Algernon Sydney and the more profound and influential John Locke were seventeenth-century English political philosphers.

[7] For an extended discussion of the terms republic and democracy, and of the relationship between liberty and democracy, see Chapter III, especially pp. 68-70.

[8] For a somewhat different but illuminating account, see the chapter on the Declaration of Independence in Harry V. Jaffa, *Crisis of the House Divided* (Garden City, N.Y.: Doubleday & Co., 1959).

[9] See Martin Diamond, "Conservatives, Liberals, and the Constitution," in R. A. Goldwin, ed., *Left, Right, and Center* (Chicago: Rand McNally & Co., 1965).

[10] *Federalist* 10, pp. 80-81.

[11] *Federalist* 37, p. 226.

[12] "Reflections on the Revolution in France," in *The Writings and Speeches of Edmund Burke* (Boston: Little, Brown & Co., 1901), III, 397-98.

Chapter 2

FRAMING THE
MORE PERFECT UNION

It is new in the history of society to see a great people turn a calm and scrutinizing eye upon itself when apprised by the legislature that the wheels of its government are stopped, to see it carefully examine the extent of the evil, and patiently wait two whole years until a remedy is discovered, to which it voluntarily submitted without its costing a tear or a drop of blood from mankind.

—TOCQUEVILLE[1]

The framing of the Constitution was one of the country's profoundly determinative political events. Major themes of the American polity were there writ large. Often in the history of nations, some single moment or event has enduring significance and consequence. In these moments when the very nature of the regime may hang in the balance, its key forces and issues are peculiarly visible. For example, to understand modern French politics one still must understand the French Revolution; similarly, to understand Soviet Russia one must understand the October Revolution of 1917. The fundamentals of a nation's polity are seen clearly in the historical setting of its decisive event. Political things are deepest, grandest, and most instructive in these great moments when the fundamental principles and structures of a regime are being determined. These moments of political creation disclose what time and the confusion of ordinary affairs tend to obscure. The framing of the Constitution is such a moment for the American polity.

Many mistakenly think of the Constitution of 1787 as belonging to a rustic America now rendered remote by the changes in American society. But think how remote 1787 is to other nations. The study

15

of, say, modern Russian, Chinese, or Ghanaian government doubt-
less profits by some reference to the late eighteenth-century politics
of those countries, but in 1787, Catherine the Great ruled in Russia,
a Manchu emperor ruled in China, and Ghana did not exist. Catherine and the Manchu would find their countries incomprehensible
today; in comparison, James Madison would be practically at his
ease in modern America. The Constitution of 1787 is still the
fundamental document of the American polity; it still embodies its
fundamental principles; it is still the legal source of its basic institutions and powers, and it still influences the politics of their operation. Despite enormous *social* and *economic* change, the
constitutional system imparts to America a remarkable *political*
continuity. Accordingly, it is not merely filial piety but sound
political science to study carefully the Convention at which the
Constitution was framed.

PREPARATIONS

Reflecting the growing support for substantial change of the
Articles, every state (except debtor-dominated Rhode Island) sent
delegations to the Convention. As under the Articles, there was no
thought of direct popular election to this 'confederal' gathering: The
state legislatures appointed the delegates.[2] The delegates therefore
largely reflected the popular political balance of the moment as it
was expressed in the basically democratic state legislatures.
Seventy-four men were named (this included numerous alternates),
and fifty-five actually attended. Of these, as many as forty took an
active part in the proceedings. The outstanding fact is that more
than forty men from all over the country worked hard and intimately during a long hot summer in Philadelphia.

The Delegates

The intellectual quality of the delegates, especially of the leading
men, was extremely high. They were adequate to the very great task
our tradition rightly deems them to have performed.[3] Most were
intelligent, many were well educated, a few were profound, and
nearly all were experienced in public and private affairs. Men like

Franklin, Madison, Hamilton, Wilson, Livingston, and Mason were scholars, authors of important works, well read in political literature, and accustomed to bring to political matters the style and penetration of their training and intellect. Madison had prepared for the Convention by making extensive historical and philosophical studies of problems that would arise; his long memorandum on the history of confederacies is still of intrinsic scholarly merit. In short, much of the country's best intelligence, experience, and reputation was at the Convention. We would understand much if we knew why there was then so little separation between power and merit, why the country's best men were called upon or were able to assume such authority.

These able men were generally quite young, averaging just over 40 years old. Indeed many of the most important delegates were among the younger men, like Charles Pinckney (29), Alexander Hamilton (32), Edmund Randolph (34), Gouverneur Morris (35), and James Madison (36). George Washington was then only 55. Yet consider the delegates' extensive experience in public service:

 6 signed the Declaration of Independence

24 served in the Continental Congress

21 fought in the Revolutionary War

46 served in colonial or state legislatures

10 helped draft state constitutions

 7 served as state governors

 6 signed the Articles of Confederation

39 served in the Confederal Congress

 3 served as Confederal administrative officers

Clearly they had had ample opportunity to learn what experience could teach about the problems that confronted the Convention. It was no small further advantage that many had come to know each other in public life, making it that much easier for the Convention to achieve profitable discussion.

In addition to possessing intellectual stature and public experience, they also were experienced in business and economic matters. Such combinations of competencies, rare today, were more common then. Of the 55 delegates: 40 owned public securities; 14 speculated in land; 24 lent money at interest; 11 had mercantile, manufacturing, or shipping connections; 15 operated plantations. Thus, most were personally involved in the economic interests that would be affected by the Convention's decisions. . . .

About one-half of the delegates were lawyers. Legal education then was sometimes rough and ready, but their practice of the law fostered the respect for precedent, procedure, and precision which the study and practice of the common law has the capacity to instill. Moreover, some delegates like Mason, Wilson, Dickinson, and Wythe were learned and distinguished lawyers by any standard. The delegates' legal habits deeply influenced the style of the Constitution.[4]

THE OPENING OF THE CONVENTION: CRUCIAL DECISIONS ON PROCEDURE

On the scheduled second Monday in May only the local Pennsylvania and the eager Virginia delegations were in attendance, but by May 25 seven states were adequately represented. The very first action taken was a revealing departure. Under the Articles, congressional action required a majority of nine states. The Convention, however, decided that seven were sufficient for a quorum—with the implication that a majority of four could act. This procedural decision at one stroke increased the likelihood of constructive action. Now no one or two state delegations could deadlock the Convention (as Maryland had held up the Articles). By making action possible, the decision encouraged a readiness to engage in practical compromise.

The Convention then unanimously elected Washington as its presiding officer. His immense personal authority made him a powerful support for the forces pressing for radical change. As behooved the chairman, and perhaps so as not to squander his influence, Washington took little open part in floor controversies. He nonetheless made his opinions known informally and, of course, by the way he voted within the Virginia delegation. His demonstrated ability to combine republican simplicity with the stern conduct of great affairs must have made it hard for delegates to exhibit frivolous or selfish objections in his presence. A Major Jackson was then appointed Secretary. Were his meager minutes all we had, we would know little of what went on. Most of our knowledge is based on the work of James Madison who, by what must have been a prodigious effort, took hundreds of pages of magnificent notes.[5] Several other delegates also kept notes and records. Madison's notes have been checked against these sources, and the story of the Convention has probably been pieced together with great accuracy.

The Basic Agreement on Procedure

Madison's account of the first day ends with this entry: "The appointment of a Committee . . . to prepare *standing rules and orders* was the only remaining step taken on this day" [May 25]. Establishing procedural rules was by no means a merely technical matter. *How* things were done would influence *what* things were done. Indeed, no procedure is so trivially technical that it may not influence a crucial outcome. That is why so many great political fights occur over such procedural matters as the size of a committee, the order of floor discussion, or the method of voting.

There were no such quarrels at the Convention. The rules were adopted with little discussion or amendment. Yet had any delegates—all of whom were connected with conflicting regional, state, economic, and religious interests—been determined to defend those interests at all costs, they would have known how to use the rules question to stall the proceedings. The amicable unity on procedure, therefore, bespeaks a quite general agreement that the fate of union was at stake. It suggests also how much the delegates had in common at the outset, how much they shared the underlying political agreement which was the product of the colonial experience. At times the Convention veered toward grave disagreement, toward what we may call *regime* politics—i.e., toward profound differences regarding the very nature of the political system, such as characterized the French Revolution. But such differences were made less likely by what the delegates believed in common. Nearly all accepted that the new government must secure liberty and yet conform to the popular genius of the country. This underlying agreement on republican liberty paved the way for full agreement or, where agreement failed, for practical compromise.

The Issue of Voting Procedure

One procedural dispute, however, was only barely averted. It foreshadowed the difficult problem that the Constitution had finally to resolve: the place of the states in the national system. The dispute was over the Convention's method of voting. The Pennsylvania delegation wanted to refuse

> the small states an equal vote, as unreasonable, and as enabling the small states to negative every good system of Government, which must in the nature of things, be founded on a violation of that equality. [But] the members from Virginia, conceiving that such an attempt might beget fatal altercations between the large and small states, and that it would be easier to prevail on the latter, in the course of the deliberations, to give up their equality for the sake of an effective Government, than on taking the field of discussion to disarm themselves of the right and thereby throw themselves on the mercy of the large states, discountenanced and stifled the project [May 28].

Pennsylvania wanted to base voting on population or wealth; Pennsylvania and Virginia (then the two largest states) would thus have between them nearly one third of the Convention's total vote. Contrarily, equal state voting would give them only one sixth of the vote. These two large state delegations happened to favor a very powerful national government. Voting by population, Pennsylvania and Virginia would need the support of only a few other states to ram through a strongly national constitution. But the members from Virginia persuaded Pennsylvania to yield because they feared a fatal altercation, i.e., that some of the small states might simply pull out and thereby abort the Convention. Virginia saw no permanent advantage in an initial procedural victory that would outrage some of the small states. They would have to be convinced in the course of the deliberations, not outmaneuvered at the outset.[6]

Organizing the Discussion

The delegates did not consider themselves mere spokesmen for their constituents or instructed agents of interest groups; they also considered themselves *listeners* to the arguments of others. No doubt most arrived with firm opinions, but they also recognized the obligation to defend their opinions rationally and to change them upon conviction. As speaking and listening representatives, they were there to discover the long run interests of the country as well as serve the immediate interests of their constituents.

Accordingly, a proposal that all votes be officially recorded whenever requested by any member was unanimously rejected because "changes of opinion would be frequent" and "such a recorded opinion . . .would be an obstacle to a change of them on conviction." Moreover, recording the members' changing opinions would open them to subsequent political attack, "furnishing handles to the adversaries of the result" of the Convention [May 28].

Further, "every member, rising to speak, shall address the President; and whilst he shall be speaking, none shall pass between them, or hold discourse with another, or read a book, pamphlet or paper, printed or manuscript" [May 28]. The Convention was not to degenerate into vain speechmaking, relegating decision to backroom maneuvers: the discussion itself was to be the real center of the Convention. Other rules made it easy to table matters or bring them back to the floor, thus avoiding procedural rigidity likely to hinder the ripening of agreement through discussion.

The Convention even took the drastic step of closing its doors: no visitors, no journalists, not even out-of-doors discussion within the earshot of non-delegates. Those who suspected the Convention would produce a strong central government naturally complained that only conspirators and evil-doers needed secrecy. Even Jefferson in Paris, who thought the Convention "an assembly of demigods," complained of the "abominable . . . precedent . . . of tying up the tongues" of the delegates.[7] The delegates defended themselves on the ground that they were only making proposals and that a full public debate would subsequently precede action.

The necessity of secrecy to some aspects of governing conflicts with the openness necessary to a liberal democracy. Openness is necessary so that voters can judge issues and persons. Moreover, public debates educate and improve public judgment. But secrecy is frequently better for producing results. One famous, but specialized, form of this problem occurs in diplomacy. For example, President Woodrow Wilson proposed "open covenants of peace, openly arrived at." Others deride this view, arguing that nations reach better agreements through closed-door negotiations where real give-and-take can occur. The problem arises in many forms, and democratic statesmanship has frequently to balance the rival claims of secrecy and openness.

In any event, the Convention never wavered from its decision for secrecy, and secrecy achieved its object. Free from daily fear of what enemies back home would make of each position taken in debate, delegates could move more freely toward whatever conclusions the course of the argument dictated.[8] The procedural decision probably had an immense substantive consequence. Had the Convention been open to public and press, it probably would not so radically have abandoned the Articles in favor of the daringly national Constitution.

THE ISSUE OF FEDERALISM

The Convention was forced to face immediately its key issue, the one that troubled it longest, most threatened to divide it, and finally was settled by its most ingenious compromise—the issue of federalism.

The Virginia Plan and a Legal Question

The federalism issue was raised by the presentation of the Virginia Plan, a detailed scheme of government carefully prepared in advance by the Virginia delegation, especially by James Madison. The outstanding fact is that the Virginia Plan proposed a radically *national* government armed with great authority. Indeed the Virginia Plan largely ignored the Articles of Confederation, despite the common expectation that the Convention would merely propose revisions to improve the existing Confederation. This raised a legal question which troubled the Convention and which has troubled some scholars since. Was the Constitution produced by a body that illegally and unethically exceeded its authority?[9]

The Convention's legal basis lay in the congressional resolution establishing it and in the states' instructions to their delegates. Delegates hostile to the radically national Virginia Plan buttressed their case with an argument drawn from the congressional resolution, which said that the Convention was called "for the sole and express purpose of *revising* the Articles of Confederation." But the Virginia Plan did not revise, it scrapped the Articles. Therefore, these delegates kept complaining that the Virginia Plan was not only undesirably national, but illegal in the first place. However, the congressional resolution also had wording that supporters of the Virginia Plan could use. It said that the *reason* for revision was "to render the federal constitution *adequate* to the exigencies of Government and the preservation of the Union." Virginia could therefore argue that the Convention was justified in going beyond revision, since that was necessary to provide an adequate government.

Both sides could make an argument upon the basis of the authorizing documents because they contained an ambiguity, indeed a contradiction. And contradiction cannot command. The contradiction lurked in the double injunction laid upon the Convention: Provide an adequately strong union and also preserve the confederal form. But what if such a union required abandoning confederation and forming a national government? Which of the two parts of the contradictory command would be binding on the Convention then? The nationalist supporters of the Virginia Plan took advantage of the contradiction to defend a plan which ignored the Articles. And the nationalists, as we shall see, throughout the Convention took advantage of the contradictory desire of their opponents for both the blessings of close union and those of loose confederal form.

The Constitution as finally adopted greatly departed from the boldly introduced Virginia Plan. But it became a sort of first draft for the Convention's discussions, and it left its imprint on the final document as first drafts often do. Madison had done his homework. He had prepared a detailed proposal and had organized the support for it. Those least willing to depart from the Articles had failed (or were unable) to organize themselves around a specific set of proposals. From the outset, therefore, the Convention found itself much farther along the road to a national government than would otherwise have been the case.

National or "Merely Federal"?

The Virginia Plan's opening wording made starkly explicit the issue so abruptly placed before the Convention. Resolved: "that a Union of the States *merely federal* will *not* accomplish the objects proposed by the articles of Confederation, namely security of liberty, and general welfare" [May 30]. Therefore "a *national* Government ought to be established consisting of a supreme Legislative, Executive and Judiciary" [May 30]. A "merely federal" union of the states *versus* a national and supreme government—for five weeks this issue held the stage. The detailed work of the Convention, the give and take of compromise from which the Constitution emerged, could not proceed until this issue was somehow settled.

How federalism is understood today. "Merely federal"? Something here confuses the ear because it runs counter to a now widely accepted classification of forms of government. Most modern writers regard the United States today as the example of a fully federal system. These writers have in mind a three-fold classification.

At one extreme is a *confederation,* a loose association of states (in older times, cities) who, as it were, are the citizens of the central body they create. They retain all the sovereign power, with the central body entirely dependent legally upon their will. In this form, . . . the states as such and not people are represented in the central body, the states vote there as equal citizens, and central decisions reach real citizens only through the states. Political life therefore centers in the separate states and not in the whole. At the other extreme is *national* or *unitary* government. Here all sovereign power rests in the central government, with localities legally entirely dependent upon its will. States are legally mere *departments*—the very word used, for example, in France—of the national government, and are its creatures. (In some unitary governments, like Britain, localities nonetheless become politically important, and power is effectively decentralized in practice.) Federal government is the third form, in this modern typology, standing between the two extremes, and presumably combining the best confederal and national features.

But when the Convention opened, there was no thought of the mixed form we now call federal. Indeed, the very words federal and confederal had not yet become distinguished; they were used synonymously. Accordingly, the delegates thought only of two mutually exclusive alternatives: confederal or federal association *versus* national government. Gouverneur Morris expressed this general view when he "explained the distinction between a *federal* and *national, supreme* government; the former being a mere compact resting on the good faith of the parties; the latter having a complete and compulsive operation" [May 30]. In short, the original intention of the leading Framers, all of whom supported the Virginia Plan, was to establish a fully national government.

The small-republic issue. On May 30 the Convention voted six states to one against a merely or purely federal plan and for the Virginia Plan's "national, supreme government." But this drastic decision could not stand. The New York delegation was split over the question and several delegations hotly opposed to a national government were only just arriving. As Madison had seen earlier, there was no point in railroading anything through; a really workable constitution would need the convinced support of nearly all the states. That kind of support could come only after long and thoughtful discussion—the kind the rules provided for—because the federal-national question involved an underlying theoretical issue: the question of the small republic.

The small-republic issue [see pg. 127] underlay the controversy over the Virginia Plan. Many delegates strongly opposed radical departure from the Articles because they believed that republicanism was doomed in a large nation. They believed therefore that small-republican states should unite only in the confederal form and primarily for defense against external enemies. Speaking from this small-republic point of view, Sherman of Connecticut argued that "the objects of Union . . . were few." Keeping the peace among the states and defending all of them against foreign enemies, he continued, "alone rendered a confederation of the States necessary. All other matters civil and criminal would be much better in the hands of the States. *The people are more happy* in small than large States" [June 6].

Madison pounced on Sherman's claim that relatively little was wanted from union. On the contrary, he argued, a central government must provide broadly and "effectually for the security of private rights and the steady dispensation of Justice." Madison then compellingly reminded the delegates that

> interferences with these were evils which had more perhaps than anything else produced this Convention. Was it to be supposed that republican liberty could long exist under the abuses of it practiced in some of the States [June 6]?

Madison was skillfully playing off two sets of fears and thus reaching into the contradiction in his opponents' position. Those who feared strong national government also feared the Shaysite drift of the individual states under the Articles. Like Madison and the nationalists, they too wanted to protect property and achieve political stability. In Chapter 3 we shall see whether these fears and aims affected the place of democracy in the Constitution. Here we are concerned only to see how Madison extorted acquiescence to a relatively strong national government from the reluctant small republicans. He drove them to admit that what they wanted from union could only be supplied by *an essentially national government.* Madison pointed out that they could not have their cake and eat it too, that they could not secure *national* benefits while retaining all the *confederal* privileges of state sovereignty.

Madison then presented the 'large-republic' argument for which he is famous. He argued that there was, in a sense, a way to have and also eat the cake—to secure *both* national benefits and republicanism *without* clinging to the purely federal form. A "merely federal" system was necessary only if republics had to be small. If republican liberty could be shown secure in a large country, then there was no longer reason to keep the system purely federal and thus weak. Madison went even further. Largeness was not only compatible with republicanism, he convincingly argued, but it was *necessary* to it. That is, he urged the very converse of the small-republic argument. He argued that smallness and not largeness caused the fatal diseases of republics. The small republics of antiquity were wretched nurseries of destructive conflicts of economic classes. Just such conflict was making liberty unsafe in the small American states; indeed, as all the delegates knew, fear of that conflict was an important reason the Convention had been called. Only a nation as large as the whole thirteen states or larger, Madison argued, would be a safe dwelling place for republican liberty.

The analysis of how the large republic functions is delayed until Chapter 3, where it may be presented more effectively. It suffices for the present discussion of the federal-national issue to state that Madison compellingly suggested ways in which the dangerously concentrated political struggles of small republics would be safely fragmented and dispersed in a large republic. He clearly modified the theoretical opinions of his opponents. In particular, Madison seems to have influenced the Connecticut delegates Ellsworth and Sherman, and it was the Connecticut delegation, as we shall see, that helped bring about the key compromise of the Convention.

The New Jersey Plan

The character and fate of what is known as the New Jersey Plan reveals how successfully Madison undermined the purely federal position. When the Virginia Plan was on the verge of decisive approval, Patterson of New Jersey presented a plan "purely federal, and contradistinguished" from the nationalist Virginia Plan [June 14]. The New Jersey Plan shows how far beyond the old Articles the antinationalists were now prepared to go. The New Jersey Plan provided for a kind of central executive and judiciary; gave Congress authority over foreign and interstate trade; gave the Union an independent revenue source; made all central laws and treaties "the supreme law of the respective states"; and empowered the central executive to use the armed might of the Confederacy to compel compliance of recalcitrant states. All this went very far indeed, and the last provision for military coercion was an amazing grant of power. It proved, however, the Achilles heel of the New Jersey Plan.

The fear that a powerful national government would destroy liberty had pushed the Convention close to a gravely divisive issue. But now the long discussion of fundamentals neared its climax and resolution. The 'pure federalists' now admitted how broad the governing powers must be to achieve the blessings of union, and that legislative, executive, and judicial organs of government were needed for their application. But the Virginia Plan advocates pointed out that the attempt to achieve these things by *purely federal means* was doomed to failure. It led—in the antinationalist New Jersey Plan—to the palpably unacceptable reliance upon military coercion. To coerce a powerful state would be in effect to engage in civil war. The best solution the pure federalists could find required a method that would "bring confusion and ruin upon the whole" [June 19]. This fatal flaw demonstrated that there was no way to have both firm union and pure federalism.

On June 19 the Convention therefore voted (7-3) against the purely federal New Jersey Plan. It may seem that the Convention had now decided for a purely national plan and that, unaccountably, we have all mistakenly called the United States a federal government. Not so. The Convention *had* once and for all turned against a purely federal system, but it had *not* thereby acquiesced in a purely national government. Compromise—a mixture of the federal and national principles — now became possible.

Political compromise occurs, it is often thought, when each side believes that it has gotten as much as it can get. True, but each side must also believe that 'as much' is enough. If men regard the proposed compromise as morally disgusting or inadequate to safeguard vital interests, they may not settle for it. They may abandon the whole process of peaceful discussion and bargaining and may seek by force to gain their whole end, or may even prefer to go down fighting rather than settle. In short, for both sides to regard a compromise as a good enough settlement, they must not be in great disagreement over a vital issue.

The Convention had originally divided over the theoretical question of federalism versus nationalism, the small-republic true federalists regarding nationalism as fatal to liberty, the nationalists regarding a purely federal system as " imbecilically" incompetent. Compromise would have been impossible across this gulf. But by undermining the small-republic theory, Madison had narrowed the conflict. He had lessened the pure federalist fear of a national government. No longer adamantly convinced that liberty was at stake, they were less adamantly opposed to nationalism. The Convention now had a different, less grave division. It was now divided between those still advocating a purely national plan and those who, having abandoned a purely federal scheme, were determined only to work some federal features into the final outcome. The distance between the two views had become compromisable, and the work of practical politics could begin.

But this was one time that the clash of theory had to precede practical politics. Indeed, the most shrewdly compromising practical politician is hopelessly inadequate when men are divided on profound theoretical issues. To be practical, politics must always presuppose underlying theoretical agreement; and the failure of practical politicians almost always is a clue to underlying theoretical disagreement. The Convention supplies a remarkable example of how theoretical agreement can be reached, and how theoretical matters govern the disposition of practical matters.[10] The Framers were theorist-politicians in the grandest manner.

The Connecticut Compromise

Once it was felt that a significantly powerful government had to be formed and could somehow safely be formed, there proved to be broad agreement on two features of the Virginia Plan: First, that a powerful government necessitated the safeguard of a bicamerally divided legislature; second, it seemed natural and necessary that at least one house be distinctly national, directly elected by the citizens, and proportioned to population, as were all the state lower houses.

But a fresh crisis broke out over the question of how to constitute the second house. The Virginia Plan's second house was completely unfederal; senatorial representation, like that in the House of Representatives, was based on population and excluded the states as such. All the pure federal fears came to fever pitch again over the question of the second house. The harassed small republicans made their last stand on this issue. Delegations threatened to desert the Convention. Even talk of the sword was heard. One side threatened to unify the country by force; the other threatened that the small states might "find some foreign ally . . . who will take them by the hand and do them justice"[11] [June 30].

At this critical juncture, on the morning of June 29, the respected Dr. Johnson of Connecticut took the floor:

> Those on one side [consider] the States as districts of people composing one political Society; those on the other [consider] them as so many political Societies, *and* a government is to be formed for them in their political capacity, as well as for the individuals composing them. Does it not seem to follow, that if the States as such are to exist they must be armed with some power of self-defense. [Therefore] the two ideas . . . instead of being opposed to each other, ought to be combined; that in *one* branch the *people*, ought to be represented; in the *other* the *States*.

Johnson's Connecticut colleague Ellsworth supported the proposal, hoping "it would become a ground of compromise. . . . We were *partly national; partly federal. . . .* He trusted that on this middle ground a compromise would take place" [June 30].

Virginia and Pennsylvania were bitterly unhappy and feared that this single federal element—a Senate federally based upon the states—would be enough to ruin the new system. But the Great or Connecticut Compromise was adopted and the crisis of the Convention was overcome. Complex political struggles often come down to some single issue in which all the passions, all the forces find their focus. When that single issue is settled it is as if all the passions and forces are spent. Both sides seem somehow obliged fully to accept the outcome and matters move quickly thereafter. In any event, so it was at the Convention. When the pure federalists gained their point on the second branch, they never again waged a general battle on the question of federalism. Indeed they seemed to vie thereafter with the nationalists in granting broad national powers to the new government.

The peculiar American brand of federalism could now be created. More accurately, as Madison later put it in *Federalist* 39, the Convention could now create a Constitution which was "in strictness neither a national nor a federal Constitution, but a composition of both."[12]

A Note on the Small- Large-State Conflict

The delegates were, of course, not disembodied intellects seeking only the light of truth. All had constituents and states with special interests to defend. During the first half of the Convention, the many interests seemed to resolve into two blocs—the large states versus the small. The large states seemed to line up behind the national Virginia Plan, the small states behind the purely federal New Jersey Plan. Indeed, traditionally they are referred to as the large- and small-state plans. Yet almost immediately after the Connecticut Compromise, the two blocs dissolved, and the bitter conflict between large and small states practically vanished. The sudden disappearance of so apparently sharp a conflict has been puzzling. The answer is that the conflict was more apparent than real or, at least, more limited than has been thought.

For one thing, the Convention did not in fact divide neatly between large and small states. The Virginia and Pennsylvania delegations, representing the two largest states, did indeed fight for national government, while very small Delaware and New Jersey resisted them. But other states did not fit the pattern. Large Massachusetts wavered; large New York sided with Delaware and New Jersey; small Georgia took the national side; and middling Connecticut and South Carolina were on opposite sides. Moreover, there were men on both sides of the question within nearly every delegation. Further, it was the temporary fortunes of politics, not the size of the states, that gave the nationalists control of the Virginia and Pennsylvania delegations. The *delegations* were nationalist; the two *states* were not. In fact, Virginia later barely ratified the Constitution.

Yet it is true that many small-state delegates vehemently protested that the large states wanted a national government because they could dominate it. Their protestations were no doubt partly genuine, but were also partly contrived. The thing to notice is this: The cry against the large states was made only by small-state delegations dominated by pure federalists; other small-state delegations made no such protestations. In short, the cry against large-state domination was partly another argument seized upon by the small-republicans [who were therefore pure federalists] to use against the nationalists.

Despite the inconclusive evidence on which it rested, the idea of a large-small state division has been widely accepted because it was erroneously thought to be the natural division. That is, large states were supposed to want close union (with voting by population), the better to dominate small states, while the latter were supposed to prefer loose confederacy (with voting by states), the better to resist. Scholars neglected Madison's correct observation that history belied this view. In the loose Greek confederacies, he pointed out, "the strongest cities corrupted and awed the weaker," and in the loose German confederacy, the small states were "exceedingly trampled upon" [June 28]. Powerful Virginia, Madison pointed out, could actually better dominate her small neighbors under the ineffectual Articles than under a national government.

The small-state complaint at the Convention was untenable because it did not reflect the true interests of the small states. It was produced by the rhetoric of those resisting the formation of a stronger central government on other grounds, namely, a small-republic theory of federalism. Once that theoretical issue had been largely resolved by the Connecticut Compromise, the small state-large state conflict proved itself of little significance and quietly faded away.

Why did scholars so readily accept the view that the small state-large state conflict was natural and fundamental? First, they seemed to regard interests—and not opinions or beliefs—as the fundamental stuff of politics; thus the idea of a massive conflict between small and large states seemed entirely plausible and needed no further reflection. Second, they treated the arguments about the issue as merely rival rationalizations of opposing interests. Thus they did not take the arguments seriously enough to evaluate their content; but such an evaluation would have disclosed the essential spuriousness of the small-state argument. Finally, and similarly, scholars have largely ignored the fundamental theoretical issue which illumines the small state-large state matter as it illumines so many other matters at the Convention, namely, the small-republic issue.

To summarize, men act not only on the basis of their economic and other interests, but out of the logic of their political opinions. Both interests and opinions are independent causes of political behavior; this methodological view is fundamental to this book.

"A BUNDLE OF COMPROMISES"?

Besides the Connecticut Compromise (often called the Great Compromise), there were many others. Indeed, Professor Max Farrand once rightly described the Constitution as a "bundle of compromises," and his phrase has won wide usage. But conflicting and erroneous conclusions can be drawn from the compromising spirit of the Convention that lead in turn to erroneous conclusions about the constitutional system.

Some have argued that the delegates' readiness to compromise proves they were really concerned only with their economic interests and thus readily abandoned political principle whenever compromise advanced those interests. On this view, the Framers were 'wheelers and dealers,' rationalizing handy principles whenever it suited their real concern—power for themselves and advantage for their interests. On the other hand, some have praised the readiness to compromise as showing a healthy disdain for principle, a sound shying away from doctrinaire philosophizing in favor of hard-headed practicality. Others have argued that, because it embodies so many compromises, the Constitution could not be logical or consistent. And because of this alleged illogicality and inconsistency, still others have tended to treat the Constitution as an obsolete eighteenth-century hodge-podge that cannot be a clear guide for the present.

But the mere fact of compromise is not proof that principle, theory, and consistency were abandoned. Rather, this book argues that the leading Framers successfully balanced the rival claims of theory and practical necessity. Despite the compromises which produced it, the Constitution is an essentially logical and consistent document resting upon a political philosophy that remains profoundly relevant.

Men of principle may properly make compromises when the compromises adequately preserve fundamental principle. We have already seen how this worked out in the dramatic Connecticut Compromise. In general, the Convention 'split the difference' only when the difference no longer involved fundamental principles. Under the pressure of necessity, men may honorably settle for less than they believe perfect. Everything depends upon whether fundamental objectives have been attained, and fundamental principles preserved, sufficiently and as completely as possible. Not the mere fact of compromise, but the *kind* of compromise gives the measure of a politician.

Another fact which minimizes the significance of the constitutional compromises is the Convention's underlying agreement on the need for popular and free institutions consistent with the 'genius' or spirit of the country. Once the federal question was settled, that agreement was all the greater. That underlying agreement contributed to the Constitution's coherence. The compromises fit within the basically consistent outlook that made the compromises possible in the first place.

Moreover, most of the compromises were over matters of detail which principle can never wholly settle, for example, the exact length of term for members of the House of Representatives. Those most concerned to keep government responsive to the people wanted a one-year term, others more concerned for stability wanted a three-year term. Yet all agreed on a stable representative body responsible to the electorate, and no one could prove exactly how long the term should be. If only a year, why not a more democratic six months; if three years, why not a more stable four years? This could reasonably be settled by compromise as could the age requirements for various offices, the ratio of representatives to inhabitants, and other like matters. Such splitting the difference does not render the Constitution a patchwork of inconsistent items.

This is not to say, however, that the Constitution is the perfectly consistent expression of complete agreement on political and legal theory. The Convention had followed Franklin's advice: when the "planks" had not fit, a little was taken from both to make "a good joint" [June 30]. And some of the joints are rough. But compromise is the creature of necessity and of men able to recognize necessity. Not blinded by a conviction of their own infallibility, and driven by a sense of urgency, the delegates compromised and were entitled rationally to hope that the Union was being made sufficiently more perfect. Because of the *kind* of compromises they made—namely, compromises basically consistent with principles—the Framers demonstrated, to modify an old expression, that politics is the art of the *best* possible.

THE SECTIONAL PROBLEM

Skill at compromise was especially needed for problems arising from sectional differences. The differences that had plagued the Confederation did not disappear at the Convention in a burst of patriotic zeal. All other things being equal, delegates still preferred that *their* interests, *their* constituents, *their* state or section enjoy any benefits available, and they coolly considered each clause with an eye to its effect upon interests with which they were immediately connected. Among these, sectional interests were especially important.

For example, Madison belittled the large-small state conflict, pointing out the greater importance of sectional conflict:

> States were divided into different interests not by their difference of size, but by other circumstances; the most material of which resulted partly from climate, but principally from the effects of their having or not having slaves. These causes concurred in forming the great division of interests in the United States. It did not lie between the

large and small states: *It lay between the Northern & Southern* [June 30].

The new government and its policies could affect the sections very differently indeed. The Constitution's procedures would give influence to one or another section. The North and the South engaged in a kind of jockeying for position at the start of the race. But at the Convention the sectional issue involved only limited economic matters. Bitter moral and political differences came to the fore only later, leading to the "irrepressible conflict" of the Civil War. Therefore, sectionalism kept the Convention busy but not profoundly agitated. Since only limited economic matters—who would get a bit more or less—and not fundamental political principles were usually involved, the conflicts were readily compromisable. Yet these were the very compromises that could not be achieved under the Articles. Daily political behavior, under the influence of the Confederation's centrifugal tendencies, steadily worsened conflicts. But here at the Convention, faced with the task of founding a government, the delegates took a less narrow view of what Franklin called their "little partial local interests" [June 28].

Slavery and the Three-Fifths Compromise

Slavery was of course the profoundest sectional problem. The Convention, however, was not deeply divided over it. Nearly all agreed that it was an unhappy inheritance from the colonial period. North and South alike hoped and expected that, as the South became more diversified agriculturally and more commercial, slavery would gradually die out. (For example, George Washington had sponsored a Potomac Canal company in order to open Virginia to the western trade. A more commercialized Virginia, he hoped, would then find slavery unprofitable and sensibly get rid of it.) The Convention knew that slavery would ultimately cause a divided nation because, perhaps immoral anywhere, it was peculiarly undesirable in a republic; slavery fostered political attitudes and habits of mastery inimical to republicanism, and a contempt for honest toil inimical to a commercial republic.

The Constitution subtly but strikingly reveals the Convention's hostile view of slavery: The word slave never appears in it. Fugitive slaves are euphemistically referred to as "Persons held to Service or Labour" (Art. IV, sec. 2). Imported slaves are described as "such Persons as any of the states now existing shall think proper to admit" (Art. I, sec. 9). As Patterson of New Jersey said, in another connection, they "had been ashamed to use the term 'slaves' and had substituted a description" [July 9]. The Convention did not want the Constitution stained with the word after the thing itself had long disappeared. And when the thing did not disappear, when the South had become more extensively and passionately committed to slavery, what the Convention did still had consequences. In the great debate of 1850, Daniel Webster was able to brandish the Constitution's shamed avoidance of the word as a rebuke to defenders of slavery.

But however much the delegates thought slavery likely to disappear in the future and however much they disapproved of it, substantial economic interests had grown out of its long existence. Most southern delegates were briskly determined to protect those interests temporarily. Many northern delegates either recognized a kind of justice in the claim for protection, or accepted the necessity to accommodate some southern demands. The famous Three-Fifths Compromise was one such accommodation.

Were Negro slaves part of the population or not? It is easy to see what was at stake in this 'procedural' question. If slaves were counted as whole persons, the South would have roughly half the seats in the population-based House of Representatives; if they were not counted at all, the North would dominate the House. Many view the Three-Fifths Compromise, by which the Convention settled the matter, as a particularly crass example of 'splitting the difference.' But the Convention had in fact little alternative. The three-fifths formula had been used in several important instances under the Articles and was included almost as a matter of course in the New Jersey Plan and in one version of the Virginia Plan. The

Convention accepted this familiar formula as the basis for calculating both House representation and direct taxation.[13]

Further, it did not seem as brazen to the Convention as it does now that the South should insist that slaves were property and yet should be represented in Congress. In fact, the South did not want the slaves represented, but wanted white representation to reflect the economic value of the slaves. Because slave labor displaced free labor, the southern states had fewer free citizens than their northern counterparts and yet were as wealthy. This fact combined with the idea (then still prevalent, albeit weakening) that property was intermixed with political rights led some northern delegates to see justice in the South's demand for greater representation than its free population warranted.

Besides, northern reluctance over counting slaves toward representation disappeared when it came to counting them in matters of taxation. The Three-Fifths Compromise can cynically be considered a bargain struck by buyers and sellers: The South bought votes with tax money, and the North sold votes for tax relief. But it was a defensible bargain, necessary to make. The South would have yielded to stronger national government on no other terms. The Convention was faced with the same kind of problem that faced Lincoln later: Not striking the bargain would have freed not a single slave while it would have destroyed the possibility of union. And only a strong union, which would engender a national commercial economy, held out the hope that slavery would gradually be eliminated. It was the general expectation that slavery would ultimately wither away that rendered the compromise necessary and palatable as a temporary expedient.[14]

The Balance of the Sectional 'Package'

Five other features of the Constitution resulted from the accommodation of southern-northern differences: the delayed ban on importing slaves, the fugitive slave clause, the prohibition against export duties, provision for passage of commercial regulations by ordinary majorities, and the requirement that treaties be ratified by a two-thirds vote in the Senate.

The African slave trade was widely regarded as the most repellent single feature of slavery. Moreover, if slavery were gradually to be extinguished, stopping the slave trade was a logical first step. It was also a first step that would meet least resistance in some southern states, like Virginia, which could profit from the domestic breeding and selling of slaves. The Convention therefore fairly easily agreed to empower Congress to forbid the importation of slaves. The only question was when to make the ban effective. The states most in need of slave imports won the concession that Congress could not enact such a prohibition for twenty years (Art. I, sec. 9).

The fugitive slave clause was hardly challenged. A system of slavery is precarious if there is a place for slaves to escape to. (Compare the Berlin Wall and Communist bitterness over West Berlin.) While slavery lasted, slave states had to be granted some method for the return of fugitive slaves. Article IV, section 2 provided that an escaped "Person held to Service or Labour . . . shall be delivered up on Claim of the Party to whom such Service or Labour may be due." It was not clear whether the national government or the state to which the slave had fled was responsible for the delivery, but Congress early assumed the responsibility and maintained fugitive slave legislation. As northern antislavery sentiment mounted, the inevitably dramatic enforcement of this legislation provoked increasing bitterness.[15]

The three remaining features—the banning of export duties and the voting procedures on commercial regulation and on treaties—resulted from sectional economic and geographic differences not necessarily connected with slavery. The North was developing rapidly in commerce, industry, and population, while the South was likely for some time to remain agricultural. The manufactured goods the South needed to import would surely be subject to duties. The South feared that its agricultural exports might be made subject to duties as well. As part of the general settlement of sectional differences, the Convention agreed to an absolute prohibition against the imposition of export duties by the national government (Art. I, sec. 9).

The South similarly feared prejudicial use of the new power to regulate commerce among the states. For example, a northern-dominated government might copy the old British navigation acts and require that southern exports be carried in American-built and -manned merchant vessels, profitably owned and operated by New Englanders. Yet the southern delegates shared the general conviction that the national government had to have the commerce power. They therefore sought protection only in a procedural device—requiring a two-thirds majority for the passage of commercial regulations. This would then have given the southern section a veto over such regulation. But the Convention was determined to keep unimpaired the new government's power over the national economy, and the South had to yield. The interstate commerce power was placed among the congressional powers subject to action by ordinary majority vote (Art. I, sec. 8).

However, the Convention did accede to the South's companion demand regarding treaties. The South had vital interests in the then Spanish-controlled Mississippi and Gulf of Mexico which the North might ignore or even deliberately sacrifice. Indeed an earlier proposed treaty with England had gravely alarmed the South in just this connection. Article II, section 2, therefore, requires that treaties be made with the "Advice and Consent of the Senate," provided that "*two-thirds* of the Senators present concur."

THE CONVENTION CONCLUDES ITS BUSINESS

On July 26, 23 resolutions were sent to a specially appointed "committee of detail." After a ten-day recess (the only long break in the summer's proceedings) the Convention labored for a month on this committee's draft of the Constitution. Finally, with all controversial matters settled, only a last literary task remained. "A Committee was then appointed . . . to revise the stile of and arrange the articles which had been agreed to by the House." Hamilton,

Madison, and the equally nationalist Rufus King and Gouverneur Morris (along with Dr. William Samuel Johnson) were named to the committee. That the Convention's final task was confided to the leading nationalists testifies to their predominance at the Convention's close.

The major writing chores went to Gouverneur Morris. His performance shows how the opportunity to commit political decision to its final verbal form can be used by a skilled individual personally to influence the event. As Madison observed, "the finish fairly belongs to the pen of Mr. Morris. . . . It is true that the state of the materials . . . was a good preparation . . . but there was sufficient room for the talents and tastes stamped by the author on the face of it."[16]

Maneuvering for the Ratification Campaign

It was one thing to prepare a good constitution; it was another to get it adopted. The question of future approval had hung over the Convention throughout. Nationalists had worried about how far they could go, and their opponents had repeatedly invoked the probable opposition of the public. The outcome was genuinely in doubt. The Constitution's sweeping changes excited powerful opposition. Presently advantaged economic interests feared new national fiscal and commercial policy. State-based politicians feared they would be downgraded by the creation of a powerful national government. The old small-republic sentiment excited popular alarm that a remote and powerful central government would crush the people's liberties. We shall see how the Constitution, now revered, was then reviled and by what a narrow margin it was ratified.

Shrewd politicians always try to launch controversial projects under the most favorable auspices. In preparing for the ratification campaign, the Framers adopted two main tactical devices: to achieve the maximum appearance of unanimity at the Convention and to tilt the ratifying procedure in favor of adoption.

Achieving 'unanimity.' Broad agreement had resulted from the initial underlying agreement of the delegates, the sense of national urgency, the exhaustive discussion, the brilliant leadership, the awareness that what the Convention could not wholeheartedly agree to the country would never agree to, and the give and take of practical compromise. Now every maneuver was employed in the closing hours to persuade the few unpersuaded and hold in line the wavering delegates.

Three influential delegates, Randolph and Mason of Virginia, and Gerry of Massachusetts, had developed strong objections to the Constitution. Aware that "a few characters of consequence . . . might do infinite mischief," by rallying popular opposition, Hamilton offered himself as a good example:

> No man's ideas were more remote from the plan than his were known to be; but is it possible to deliberate between anarchy and Convulsion on one side, and the chance of good to be expected by the plan on the other [Sept. 17].

Randolph, Mason, and Gerry were not persuaded. But it happened that majorities in all eleven state delegations still in attendance were in favor of the Constitution. This suggested a ploy. The delegates were not asked to sign the document in their individual capacities (as the Declaration of Independence was signed); this would have left the names of Randolph, Mason, and Gerry embarrassingly missing. Rather it was adopted "by the unanimous consent of the *States* present. . . . In Witness whereof we have hereunto subscribed our names" (Art. VII). In this form, the Constitution went to the people with the useful appearance of unanimity stamped upon its face.[17]

The ratification procedure. The second tactical device—a loaded ratifying procedure—was far more important. Here the Convention skirted illegality. Was not a Convention which had been called to "revise the Articles" obliged to use the prescribed method of unanimous amendment? But fidelity to the Articles' procedure— approval first by Congress and then by all the state legislatures—

would have doomed the Constitution. The legislatures, dominated by politicians with a personal stake in the old arrangements, would be more hostile to the Constitution than the people. Several legislatures would surely balk at the sweeping changes proposed. The Convention decided to short-circuit these difficulties; it proposed to go directly to the people, over the heads of all the existing organs of government. Further, it made approval in only nine states sufficient for ratification; the new government would come into being at least for those nine states.

Not only tactics but a question of principle was involved. Even if all the state legislatures ratified the Constitution, the new government would be the creature of the preexisting state sovereignties. Legislative ratification would suggest that the new Constitution was but a treaty (in the old federal sense) of sovereign states, subject to the higher legal authority of the state governments which created it. What the state legislatures had joined together they could claim the authority to put asunder. In short, ratification by state governments would tend to make the system merely federal, precisely what the Convention had struggled to avoid.

For bypassing the legislatures, there was excellent precedent in the way some state constitutions had been adopted—the specially and popularly elected ratifying convention. The Convention directed Congress to submit the Constitution "to a Convention of Delegates, chosen in each State by the People thereof." This was a deft stroke for a body about to be denounced from one end of the country to the other for its highhanded and undemocratic manner and views. Opponents of the Constitution found it hard to convince their fellow-citizens that there was anything highhanded or undemocratic in letting the people and not the state legislatures make the decision.

But there was no such precedent for ignoring the Articles' requirement for unanimity and providing for ratification by only nine states. Indeed, a few have argued that the adoption of the Constitution was a kind of *coup d' état* or usurpation. Yet, although the legal status of the action was ambiguous, the free and democratic ratification debate sufficiently exonerates the Constitution from the charge.

Moreover, not *any* nine states would have sufficed for ratification in practice. Geography and political realities dictated that abstention by key states like Virginia or New York would render impractical a union of the remaining states. But the nine-state requirement prevented any single small state from obstructing the plan. (Remember how long Maryland had delayed the Articles, and remember that Rhode Island had not even been willing to participate in the Convention.) Moreover, a kind of bandwagon effect might occur: After a number of states had ratified, the recalcitrants might feel it futile to resist since solitary resistance could not automatically kill the Constitution.

THE CAMPAIGN FOR THE CONSTITUTION

"The business being thus closed, the members adjourned to the City Tavern, dined together and took a cordial leave of each other."[18] But politics had not waited politely for the Convention to conclude its business. Martin of Maryland, and Yates and Lansing of New York had long since left Philadelphia to raise up an opposition. And, secrecy notwithstanding, nationalist delegates had discreetly kept associates back home aware of what was afoot. The ratification campaign began long before there was even a draft of the Constitution.

Like other great political struggles, the campaign over the Constitution was a compound of many things that are difficult to disentangle. Four kinds of factors were predominant: state political alliances forged in earlier conflicts; economic, social, and geographic interests; the issues and arguments; the rival leaderships and maneuvers. In examining these, we continue our examination of what was writ large in this formative period of American politics. The political patterns we see here are of the kinds that continue in modern American politics. And in seeing how the Constitution was fought over, we see further into its character.

Old Political Alignments in the States

Old loyalties and obligations (and enmities) carry over into new disputes. When new issues arise, division tends inertially to occur along old party lines. So it was in the ratification campaign. The Convention itself was brought about by a loose national political coalition of men who had worked together earlier on a variety of problems. These same men led the campaign for the Constitution, while opposition to the Constitution rallied round traditional state rivals of the nationalist leaders. In Virginia, Patrick Henry and Richard Henry Lee again battled Washington, Madison, and Randolph; in New York, Schuylers and Livingstons again joined Hamilton against Governor Clinton's powerful following. To a degree, then, the ratification campaign was a continuation of old political wars.

Interest Groups: Cui Bono?

Mystery story readers ask an ancient Latin political question when they ask of a crime: *cui bono?*—roughly translated, *who benefits?* The question is almost always pertinent in politics: Who benefits from this law, that form of taxation, that method of letting defense contracts, the decision to convert this street and not that one into a throughway? This is not cynically to suggest that politics is exclusively a clash of selfish private interests. Politics also involves the deliberate pursuit of the public good. But some men do selfishly seek private advantage from politics, and most men often confuse their private interests with the public interest, unwittingly making the latter a flattering rationalization of the former. Moreover, the most disinterested justice sometimes requires special benefits for special groups. In short, such considerations of group interest are deeply and inherently involved in the subject matter of political science.

Even more than ordinary legislation, the framing of an effective constitution—the fundamental law and the basic procedures by which later law is to be made—affects the broad private interests of the community. Inevitably, therefore, it calls into play these powerful forces, and their conflict sheds light on the meaning of the constitution over which they struggle.

Charles Beard's "Economic Interpretation." The founding generation's motives and interests have frequently become a political issue. A recent example is the New Deal controversy in the 1930s, but the classic example occurred during 1880-1914. The rising reform and radical movements of that period resented the constitutional impediments to majority rule. Hoping for success in the popular House, they feared frustration by the restraining devices of the Constitution. But late nineteenth-century scholarship had virtually converted the Constitution into a divine code received at Sinai, and had deified the Founders. Such scholarship enabled the dominant conservative leadership of that period to parade as the Mosaic guardians of the constitutional tablets. Constitution-worship and veneration of the Founding Fathers had become a powerful support of the status quo. Inevitably, reformers began to search about for feet of clay, to show that the Founders were not disinterested patriots but men rigging a constitution to protect their own interests. Debunking the Founders would emancipate the present from the moral claim of the past and open the way for drastic reform proposals.

Charles A. Beard's *An Economic Interpretation of the Constitution*[19] became the classic formulation of the debunking attack. The title conveys the book's thesis: Nearly every important thing connected with the Constitution—the Convention, the provisions of the Constitution, the way it was ratified—is alleged to have an economic basis. Beard portrayed the Framers as "hard-fisted conservatives," protecting "their own interests and those of their class," by constitutionally hamstringing the democratic masses.[20] First, he dug out of neglected archives information on the *personal* economic holdings and interests of the Convention delegates. Second, he argued that those personal interests revealed a *class* pattern, that the delegates represented the wealthy classes, in particular the securities-holding, creditor, hard-money, mercantile, and large landholder interests. Finally, he argued that they deliberately designed an undemocratic

Constitution to protect these privileged economic classes. Surely, this was dethroning the Founders with a vengeance.

While Beard may have valuably reintroduced economic reality into the contemplation of the constitutional period, his evidence and inferences were faulty. Indeed, he himself came nearly to deny, and others tried to moderate, the book's implications. But for a half-century, the Constitution was studied with undue emphasis on its alleged antidemocratic tendencies and on economic determinism. New studies are refuting Beard's main contentions and undermining their influence (see bibliographic note for this chapter). The main historical refutation is that leading *opponents* of the Constitution had in fact roughly the same kinds and degrees of property as the leading *proponents.* That is, the wealthy were not unified as a class in support of the Constitution; men with the same economic interests were deeply divided politically. Indeed, one-fourth of the Convention delegates "had important economic interests that were adversely affected, directly and immediately, by the Constitution they helped write. . . . Finally, it is abundantly evident that the delegates, once inside the Convention, behaved as anything but a consolidated economic group."[21]

Moreover, whatever the economic factors, Beard's main argument falls on one major point: The Constitution is not, as he was obliged to claim, undemocratic. But this subject we examine in the next chapter.

Five main interest-group factors. If economic factors did not divide the country between rich and poor or along any clear class lines, still they figured prominently in the ratification process. Five main conclusions are emerging in modern historical scholarship. First, hard-money creditors tendered to favor the Constitution while soft-money debtors tended to oppose it. Debtors had obtained favorable state legislation and therefore feared transfer of effective fiscal power to the national government. (Remember that debtors are not necessarily poor; wealthy speculators are often the greatest borrowers.) Second, rich or poor, merchant or artisan, persons intimately connected with commerce probably favored the Constitution more than any other group. This followed from one obvious and great advantage of the new government: it would support a flourishing interstate commerce. Thus, everyone connected with commerce had a potential economic interest in the ratification of the Constitution. This is the key point: *everyone*—rich merchant *and* poor artisan. Rather than being divided along class lines by the Constitution (Beard's erroneous implication), all classes involved in commerce tended to be drawn together in support of it. This foreshadowed a truly vital feature of the American polity—a common interest in the commercial economy minimizing class political warfare.

Third, townspeople favored the Constitution more than did countryfolk. Fourth, the more settled coastal areas favored it more than did the western backcountry areas. But these two factors are probably closely correlated with the commercial factor, commerce being strongest in the towns and these chiefly located in the coastal areas. Fifth, important noneconomic interest groups, like army officers, newspaper publishers, and clergymen, probably tended to favor the Constitution.

Yet many of these tendencies were frequently reversed. Many hard-money, rich, eastern townsmen bitterly opposed, while many soft-money, poor, western farmers ardently supported, the Constitution. Local or individual tendencies sometimes overcame more general economic, social or geographic factors. Indeed, the ratification campaign resembles the complicated fragmenting and interweaving of interest groups in a modern presidential compaign. And many leading individuals were primarily moved by the sheer force of political ideas, regardless of their socioeconomic situations.

The Issues and the Arguments

Naturally, many arguments made at the Convention reappeared in the ratification compaign, but with greater partisan vehemence in the context of a popular campaign. Above all, the pure-federalist qualms and doubts, allayed by Madison at the Convention, flared up in the form of two related charges. First, those who opposed the adoption of the Constitution charged that it violated state sovereignty and created a consolidated national government; it was insufficiently *federal*. Second, they claimed it had undemocratic, dangerously oligarchic tendencies; it was insufficiently *republican*. The two charges were connected by the belief that, *because* the new system was insufficiently federal, it *must* be insufficiently republican. In short, the small-republic belief underlay the ratification debates. The prevalence of this idea becomes understandable when we remember that there was no empirical evidence yet of the feasibility of a large republic. America became the first large republic that ever was.

The small-republic suspicions were at the bottom of many specific complaints. Three typical charges, each with lively modern reverberations, illustrate this. First, members of the new House of Representatives would be insufficiently sympathetic with the interests of their constituents because, in so large a republic, each representative had to represent many thousands of citizens. (The new House was to have only 55 members, fewer even than some state legislatures.) Such a representative, according to the small-republic view, was too remote from his constituents faithfully to represent their wishes. Second, the President would employ the standing army as an engine of despotism against the people. A state governor, the reasoning ran, could be safely controlled but the remote national executive could not. Third, the new national courts would gradually displace the state courts, and national judges would be indifferent to local needs and interests. In short, every power of the new government seemed threatening when viewed through the magnifying lens of the small-republic view.

"All of us little folks." The statement of a delegate in the Massachusetts ratifying convention conveys the overall suspicion that the new government would become undemocratic. Many writers who view the Constitution as somehow undemocratic have fondly seized upon this quotation.

> These lawyers, and men of learning, and moneyed men, that talk so finely, and gloss over matters so smoothly, to make us poor illiterate people swallow down the pill, expect to get into Congress themselves; they expect to be the managers of this Constitution and get all the power and all the money into their own hands, and then they will swallow up all of us little folks, like the great *Leviathan* ...yes, just as the whale swallowed up Jonah.[22]

Unmistakably, then, the issue of democracy entered the ratification campaign. Opponents of the Constitution spoke the language of embattled defenders of popular rights, and supporters of the Constitution warned about the dangers of democracy. But to understand exactly how the question of democracy figured in the campaign, it helps to hear a fellow delegate's seldom quoted reply:

> I am a plain man, and get my living by the plough. ... [I want] to say a few words to my brother ploughjoggers. ... I had been a member of the Convention to form our own state constitution, and had learnt something of the checks and balances of power, and I found them all here. ... I don't think the worse of the Constitution because lawyers, and men of learning, and moneyed men, are fond of it. I don't suspect that they want to get into Congress *and abuse their power.* ... I think those gentlemen, who are so very suspicious that as soon as a man gets into power he turns rogue, had better look at home.[23]

This reply makes three important points. First, some supporters of the Constitution were ploughjoggers too, just as poor and plain as any of its opponents. Second, the Constitution is no unchecked Leviathan of power; it has all the checks and balances of the Massachusetts constitution, and these are enough. Finally, men are not necessarily all rogues, and power is not necessarily always abused. In short, this pro-Constitution 'ploughjogger' makes clear that the dispute over the Constitution was not a struggle between classes over *whether* to have democratic government or not. Rather, it was a dispute over *how* to establish a free and competent democratic government. How the American constitutional system answers that question is explicitly the theme of the next chapter and implicitly of the entire book.

Campaign Leadership and Maneuvers

Nationalist leaders pressed for quick action, believing that time (for doubts to multiply) would work against the Constitution. For example, several Pennsylvania state legislators opposed to the Constitution stalled proceedings by absenting themselves from the legislative session; this left the legislature two members shy of a quorum. The next day, a town mob hunted down two opposition legislators and literally carried them to their seats. The legislature promptly scheduled an election of delegates for a ratifying convention. The maneuver succeeded. Pro-Constitution delegates won in sufficient number to ratify the Constitution. Delay might have changed the outcome; only months later a political coalition hostile to the Constitution returned to power in the state.

The promise of subsequent amendments. Within five months, the early tide of pro-Constitution sentiment produced ratification by large majorities in five states. The Constitution met its first severe test in Massachusetts. The agreement that finally pulled it through helped to produce an immense consequence—the Bill of Rights.

The Massachusetts Convention was closely divided. The still influential Revolutionary leaders Sam Adams and John Hancock wavered or were unsympathetic. Shrewd political pressure by the Constitution's convention managers brought the two around. But more than manipulation of a few leaders was required. One of the ratification campaign's major tactical issues came to a head here. Just as pro-Constitution men sought quick action, anti-Constitution men sought to avoid a showdown vote. Their most powerful argument for delay was to propose a second constitutional convention; such delay, they argued, would result in a better constitution, incorporating the improvements suggested by the present public discussion. The Massachusetts pro-Constitution men produced an imaginative solution: ratify now and amend later. That is, Massachusetts ratified the Constitution (by a bare 187-168), but simultaneously recommended a series of amendments to be added later. The idea caught on and a number of states ratified in the same manner. It is entirely possible that without this understanding the Constitution would have failed in several key states.

However, no ratifications were *conditional* upon the addition of the Bill of Rights. This was so, first, because supporters of the Constitution refused to allow this mode of adoption; secondly, because many of the suggested amendments concerned parts of the plan of government, rather than the absence of sufficient protections for individual liberties. Accordingly, an ill-assorted mass of amendments was proposed: some aimed at further protections for democratic liberties, others would have changed the structure of the new government; and still others were meant to restore some of the states' sovereignty. Under the insistence and leadership of James Madison, the First Congress reduced these amendments to those now known as the Bill of Rights, or the first ten Amendments to the Constitution.

The Federalist. The two most dramatic conventions were in New York and Virginia, states without which no other group of states could hope to launch a general government. The New York campaign produced one especially significant result—*The Federalist.*[24] This was a series of 85 essays published in the New York press and then brought out as a kind of campaign handbook. It was written, under the pseudonym *Publius,* by Hamilton, Madison, and John Jay. A campaign document, written under extreme pressure of time ("with the printer's devil ever at my elbow," Madison said), *The Federalist* is, nonetheless, perhaps the finest American writing on politics. Jefferson called it "the best commentary on the principles of government which was ever written."[25] Moreover, it is the writing of men who themselves shaped the enduring principles of the American polity. We draw freely in this book from this intellectual resource.

But the brilliance of *The Federalist* notwithstanding, the Constitution seemed doomed in the hostile New York convention. It took Hamilton's performance on the floor, a threat that New York City would secede and join the Union alone, word that New Hampshire and Virginia had become the ninth and tenth states to ratify, a pledge to try to secure certain amendments, and last-minute support by Melancton Smith, an antifederalist leader, before the Constitution finally squeaked through 30-27 against the powerful local political opposition.

Ratification had involved rough and tumble maneuvering and, as Hamilton said, the play of "ambition, avarice, personal animosity, party opposition, and many other motives not more laudable than these."[26] Nonetheless the Constitution had been ratified by a high and solemn democratic procedure after a full, free, and intelligent debate. The fullness of the debate contributed much to its complete acceptance by virtually all parties and groups within a generation. Tocqueville eloquently characterized that debate:

> If America ever approached (for however brief a time) that lofty pinnacle of glory to which the proud imagination of its inhabitants is wont to point, it was at this solemn moment, when the national power abdicated, as it were, its authority. All ages have furnished the spectacle of a people struggling with energy to win its independence; and the efforts of the Americans in throwing off the English yoke have been considerably exaggerated. . . . [Indeed] it would be ridiculous to compare the American war to the wars of the French Revolution. . . . But it is new in the history of society to see a great people turn a calm and scrutinizing eye upon itself when appraised by the legislature that the wheels of its government are stopped, to see it carefully examine the extent of the evil, and patiently wait two whole years until a remedy is discovered, to which it voluntarily submitted without its costing a tear or a drop of blood from mankind.[27]

The debate over the Constitution was a climactic encounter between two rival political theories of how the ends of democratic consent, liberty, and competent government can best be attained. Despite the broad agreement reached on political fundamentals, deep cleavage was always a possibility. Men of all kinds and classes were drawn into the conflict, adhering to one variation or another of the two theories. Opponents of the Constitution held to the old view that political power had to be tied down close to home. Its supporters urged the new view that great power could safely (if carefully) be assigned to the government of an extended republic. The conflict of these views and kinds of interests—revealed so dramatically during the formative decade—is always just beneath the surface of American politics.

BIBLIOGRAPHICAL NOTE

The major sources on the Convention are available in Max Farrand, *The Records of the Federal Convention of 1787* (1911–1937); this definitive four-volume work is a careful collection of all the major notes and papers on the proceedings of the Convention. Another valuable collection is Charles C. Tansill, *Documents Illustrative of the Formation of the Union of the American States* (1927). Adrienne Koch, ed., *Notes of the Debates in The Federal Convention of 1787 reported by James Madison* is a one volume account. On the state ratifying conventions see Jonathan Elliot, *Debates in the Several State Conventions on the Adoption of the Federal Constitution* (1836–1845), and Merrill Jensen, *Documentary History of the Ratification of the Constitution* (1976–). Max Farrand, *The Framing of the Consitution* (1913), and Charles Warren, *The Making of the Constitution* (1928) are useful accounts of the Convention. A. C. McLaughlin, *A Constitutional History of the United States* (1935) is a general account of the constitutional background.

Charles Beard, *An Economic Interpretation of the Constitution* (1913) has been discussed in the chapter. For an early questioning of Beard's interpretation, see Douglass G. Adair, "Tenth *Federalist* Revisited," and " 'That Politics May Be Reduced to a Science': David Hume, James Madison and the Tenth *Federalist,*" in *Fame and the Founding Fathers* (1974). A number of books reexamining Beard's work and freshly investigating the problems have appeared recently: Robert Brown, *Charles Beard and the Constitution*

(1956), Forrest McDonald, *We the People: The Economic Origins of the Constitution* (1958), *E Pluribus Unum* (1965); Lee Benson, *Turner and Beard: American Historical Writing Reconsidered* (1960); Cushing Strout, *The Pragmatic Revolt in American History* (1958); Richard Hofstadter, *The Progressive Historians: Beard, Turner, Parrington* (1968).

For a discussion of the principles of the Constitution see R. A. Goldwin and W. A. Schambra, eds., *How Democratic is the Constitution?* (1980). A view differing from the one presented in this chapter is John P. Roche, "The Founding Fathers: A Reform Caucus in Action," *American Political Science Review* (December, 1961).

Two books of readings which contain important material on the Convention and on the topics in Chapter 3 are: Willmoore Kendall and George Carey, eds., *Liberalism and Conservatism* (1966), and Jack P. Greene, *The Reinterpretation of the American Revolution, 1763–1789* (1968).

All the antifederalist writings, as well as an analytical essay will be found in Herbert J. Storing, *The Complete Antifederalist* (1981). See also Jackson T. Main, *The Antifederalists* (1961) and Cecilia M. Kenyon, "Men of Little Faith: the Anti-Federalists on the Nature of Representative Government," *William and Mary Quarterly* 3rd ser., XII (1955). The original writings of the antifederalists are also available in Paul L. Ford, *Essays on the Constitution* (1892), and *Pamphlets on the Constitution* (1888); see also such recent collections as Morton Borden, *The Antifederalist Papers* (1965), and Cecilia M. Kenyon, *The Antifederalists* (1966). For a discussion of one antifederalist see Ann Stuart Diamond, "The Antifederalist Brutus" in *Political Science Reviewer* (1976).

On the adoption of the Bill of Rights, see Irving Brant, *The Bill of Rights* (1965) and *James Madison, Father of the Constitution* (1950); see also *Federalist* 84, and Madison's Speech of June 8, 1789 in Gaillard Hunt, *The Writings of James Madison*, V (1910) p. 370, and letter to Thomas Jefferson, Oct. 17, 1788, in Marvin

Meyers, *The Mind of the Framer* (1973). See also Herbert J. Storing, "The Constitution and the Bill of Rights," in *Essays on the Constitution of the U.S.,* M. Judd Harmon, ed. (1978). For an account of the historical development of one right see Leonard Levy, *Origins of the Fifth Amendment* (1968).

The modern view of federalism is presented in Kenneth C. Wheare, *Federal Government* (1947) and in "Federalism," by Arthur W. MacMahon, in *Encyclopedia of the Social Sciences.* The 1787 debate on federalism is discussed in essays by Walter Berns, Martin Diamond, Russell Kirk, and Herbert Storing in *A Nation of States* (Robert A. Goldwin, ed., 1963). See also "The Federalist's View of Federalism," by Martin Diamond, in George C. S. Benson, et al., *Essays in Federalism* (1961), and "The Ends of Federalism," in *Publius* (Fall 1973) and "The *Federalist* on Federalism: "Neither a National Nor a Federal Constitution, But a Composition of Both," in *Yale Law Journal* (May 1977).

The collected writings of the leading Framers, an indispensable source, are available in a number of editions. There are also many good biographies of the leading figures; the outstanding and most pertinent one is Irving Brant's six volume study of James Madison (1941-1956).

NOTES

[1] Alexis de Tocqueville (1805-1859), a French writer and statesman, visited the United States in 1831 and wrote a classic commentary on American society and politics, *Democracy in America,* 2 vols., Phillips Bradley, ed. (New York: Alfred A. Knopf, Inc., 1945) I, pp. 117-18. It is an invaluable guide to understanding the American policy. Marvin Zetterbaum, *Tocqueville and the Problem of Democracy* (Stanford: Stanford University Press, 1967), is a fine commentary on Tocqueville.

[2] South Carolina, where the governor appointed the delegation, was the sole exception.

[3] The famous observation of William Gladstone, a major British statesman of the nineteenth century, aptly expresses the common opinion: "As the British Constitution is the most subtile organism which has proceeded from the womb and the long gestation of progressive history, so the American

Constitution is, so far as I can see, the most wonderful work ever struck off at a given time by the brain and purpose of man." *North American Review,* CCLXIV (Sept.-Oct., 1878).

[4] Ever since, lawyers have predominated in American legislatures. Tocqueville thought this predominance likely in a democracy: "As the lawyers form the only enlightened class whom the people do not mistrust, they are naturally called upon to occupy most of the public stations." *Op. cit.,* I, 279. Moreover, the fact that we govern ourselves under a written constitution interpreted by a Supreme Court gives a legalistic framework to our politics, bringing lawyers naturally to the fore.

[5] "In pursuance of the task...I chose a seat in front of the presiding member....I noted in terms...intelligible to myself what was read from the Chair or spoken by the members; and losing not a moment unnecessarily between the adjournment and reassembling of the Convention I was enabled to write out my daily notes....In the labor and correctness of this I was not a little aided by practice, and by a familiarity with the style and train of observation and reasoning which characterized the principal speakers....I was not absent a single day, nor more than a casual fraction of an hour in any day, so that I could not have lost a single speech, unless a very short one." Max Farrand, ed., *The Records of the Federal Convention* (New Haven, Conn.: Yale University Press, 1911), III, 550. "Mr. Madison (said) that the labor of writing out the debates, added to the confinement to which his attendance in Convention subjected him, almost killed him; but that having undertaken the task he was determined to accomplish it." *Idem.*

Madison's notes and the other sources are all printed in *Documents Illustrative of the Formation of the Union of the American States,* selected, edited, and indexed by Charles C. Tansill (69th Cong., 1st sess.; House Doc. 398, Washington, D.C., 1927), cited hereafter as Tansill. In this chapter all quotations from the Convention proceedings are from Madison's notes and are followed by the date on which they took place.

[6] The Convention's voting procedure problem (but not its solution) is dramatically paralleled in the conflict between the U.S.S.R. and Red China. Mao Tse-tung had Pennsylvania's idea. At Communist world conferences "each of the 81 Communist parties has had one vote....The Chinese are said to have proposed that the votes of each party be weighted...by the size of the party...[and] by the size of the population it rules. This would automatically give the Chinese domination of the world Communist movement." *The New York Times,* Western Ed., July 10, 1963, p. 3.

[7] *The Writings of Thomas Jefferson,* H. A. Washington, ed. (New York, 1861), II, 260.

[8] It also had the interesting consequence that the full proceedings of the Convention were not available to the public until 1840, when James Madison's notes were posthumously published. Thus, all the great early constitutional decisions, while invoking the intent of the Framers, had to be taken without the full record of that intent.

[9] The method by which the Constitution was ratified raised a similar question in somewhat graver form (see below, pp. 43-44).

[10] See John P. Roche, "The Founding Fathers: A Reform Caucus in Action," *American Political Science Review,* LV (1961), 799, and Forrest McDonald, *We the People: The Economic Origins of the Constitution* (Chicago, 1963) for contrary interpretations of the Convention.

[11] The situation seemed so grave to Benjamin Franklin that he wrote a pacifying speech (too frail to speak himself, he had it read by a colleague), urging restraint and recommending the Convention thereafter open its daily sessions with prayer. It was immediately objected that to begin praying "at this late day" would arouse public alarm (the ministers would be seen coming and going in the mornings) and perhaps thus injure the Convention. Someone said the real reason for omitting prayers was that "the Convention had no funds" to pay ministers. The story has often been told that Hamilton opposed Franklin's motion on the ground that the Convention needed no "foreign aid." For whatever reason, the Convention evaded the issue by "silently postponing the matter by adjournment." The meetings continued without prayer [June 28].

[12] See pp. 124 ff. for extended discussion of the modern American federal system.

[13] Article I, section 2 states that "representatives and direct taxes shall be apportioned among the several States... according to their respective numbers, which shall be determined by adding the whole number of free persons... and excluding Indians not taxed, three fifths of all other persons." Notice the avoidance of the word "slave" and that free Negroes were to be counted as equal to whites.

[14] For a contrary view of this matter, see Staughton Lynd, *Class Conflict, Slavery and the United States Constitution* (New York: Bobbs-Merrill, 1967). For a convincing analysis of the slavery problem, especially as understood by Lincoln, see Harry V. Jaffa, *The Crisis of the House Divided* (Garden City: Doubleday and Co., 1959).

[15] See, for example, the case of *Ableman* v. *Booth,* 21 Howard 506 (1859).

[16] Max Farrand, ed., *The Records of the Federal Convention of 1787*, III, 499, from a letter written by Madison in 1831.

[17] In addition, George Washington's personal authority was prominently placed behind the Constitution. As chairman, he submitted the document to the confederal Congress with an impressive message that bore weight (as it was intended to do) in the subsequent public debates.

[18] *Diaries of George Washington*, John C. Fitzpatrick, ed. (Boston: Houghton-Mifflin, 1925).

[19] (New York: The Macmillan Company, 1913).

[20] Stanley Elkins and Eric McKittrick, *The Founding Fathers: Young Men of the Revolution*, American Historical Association Service Center for Teachers of History Series (New York: The Macmillan Company, 1961).

[21] Forrest McDonald, *We the People: The Economic Origins of the Constitution* (Chicago: University of Chicago Press, 1958), pp. 349-50.

[22] Jonathan Elliot, *Debates in the Several State Conventions on the Adoption of the Federal Constitution* (Philadelphia: J. B. Lippincott, 1907), II, 102.

[23] *Ibid.*, p. 103.

[24] The title is confusing: Why should nationalists like Hamilton and Madison call themselves federalists? The title was a theft. In order to take advantage of a popular political label, these leading proponents of a supreme, national government simply styled themselves federalists. The pure federalists, like Richard Henry Lee who signed his criticisms of the Constitution "Letters of a *Federal* Farmer" (italics supplied), angrily denounced the rhetorical device. But the theft was so successful that generations of scholars have since called the opponents of the Constitution the antifederalists.

[25] Letter to Madison, Nov. 18, 1788.

[26] *Federalist* 1, p. 4.

[27] *Op. cit.*, I, 117-18.

Chapter 3

THE FUNDAMENTAL
POLITICAL PRINCIPLES

I am therefore of the opinion, that social power superior to all others must always be placed somewhere; but I think that liberty is endangered when this power finds no obstacle which can retard its course, and give it time to moderate its own vehemence.

—TOCQUEVILLE[1]

This was the only defence against the inconveniencies of democracy consistent with the democratic form of Government.

—MADISON[2]

Separation of powers, bicameralism, judicial review, the Bill of Rights, federalism. How splendid, how familiar, how dull! Let us acknowledge the secret ennui that greets these words. Understandably bored by well-meant but unthoughtful repetition, most of us turn off a kind of psychic hearing aid when these constitutional principles and devices are discussed yet once again. In this chapter we describe their relationship and the underlying political ideas which they embody. When their pattern and meaning are seen, cynical boredom or unthinking acceptance may give way to the reasoned appreciation the constitutional principles and devices deserve.

Their meaning must be seen in terms of the basic aim of the political order. To summarize: The American political order is now, and has been from the outset, an attempt to achieve a free and competent "democratic form of Government." This view of the polity's fundamental aim determines this chapter's inquiries. For example: Does separation of powers actually protect liberty? If it does, is the price a fragmented government, incompetent to its modern tasks? And if the separation of powers helps keep the system both free and

61

competent, is it compatible with democracy? Or does the separation of powers frustrate majority rule? In this chapter, we examine the fundamental political principles of the Constitution to see whether they work to satisfy the aspiration of the system—a free, competent, democratic government.

"THE DEMOCRATIC FORM OF GOVERNMENT"

Whether or not the Constitution established a decisively democratic government has been the most disputed question. And for good reason. It is the ground on which all else rests because the question of democracy speaks to the fundamental nature of a regime. Accordingly, the answer to the question profoundly influences both practical politics and the way politics is studied. For example, if the Constitution is undemocratic and one believes in democracy, then the most important practical task is to alter the Constitution or get round it somehow, and the most important scientific task is to see how the Constitution is at odds with the requirements of a modern democratic system.[3]

But those who seek to alter or supersede the Constitution at least acknowledge its importance; they obviously regard the Constitution as an important influence upon contemporary American political behavior, a view which this book shares. But many other modern political scientists depreciate the significance of the Constitution as an influence upon behavior. They believe that, despite the undemocratic Constitution, the political system gradually, albeit imperfectly, became democratized. Focussing their attention on underlying sociological developments like industrializaion and urbanization, they believe that the Constitution has been democratized by the informal process of politics. The *political process* is thus treated as radically distinct from, in conflict with, and more important than *constitutional forms*. According to this view, for example, the extra-constitutional development of mass political parties and presidential popular leadership short-circuited the resistance to democracy of the eighteenth-century Constitution.

On this view, history has to repeat itself every day. The Constitution is seen as still the archaic undemocratic document of 1787. Thus the political short-circuiting must occur daily to permit the modern democratic system to function. The student of American government is therefore told that he must constantly penetrate the constitutional formal facade to find the democratic political reality behind it. Indeed, modern behavioral theory teaches that political science generally must emphasize the perennial tension between mere legal forms and underlying political reality.[4]

But what if, contrary to currently prevailing views, the Constitution was never undemocratic? What if the informal political process has been in subtle ways the natural and fulfilling response to the formal Constitution? Then the practical and scientific tasks are wholly different. This book holds that the Constitution is now, has been, and was intended by its framers to be fundamentally democratic. The constitutional forms, therefore, need not constantly be evaded or warped to permit democracy to function. Rather, the constitutional forms generate the political process and are in harmony with it. The practical task, then, is not to get round the Constitution, but to help it fulfill itself. And to study American government scientifically, we believe, is to study the complex but compatible relationship between the jointly democratic 'constitutional' and 'political' aspects of the American polity.

The Original Intention Regarding Democracy

The question whether the original Constitution was undemocratic requires examining what the Framers thought about democracy. Here and throughout the chapter we must consider their opinions in order to understand their handiwork. At first glance, the evidence suggests to the modern student that the founding generation feared democracy and hence must have rejected it and framed a nondemocratic government. It is unmistakable that most of the Framers had great fears regarding democracy. However, whether they took the step from *fear* to *rejection* is precisely the question.

All the leading Framers were familiar with the political writings of antiquity and accepted much of the classical criticism of democracy. Consider how Socrates challenged the idea of democracy. What, he asked, was the people's claim to rule? Governing or ruling, he argued, was an art like the arts of medicine or navigation. Yet in illness or peril at sea, it made no sense to take a poll of all the patients or passengers. The sensible thing, he suggested, was to seek and follow expert guidance in such matters. Why then in government, in the most important art of all, should power be given to the inexpert many instead of the expert few? The question is acute. Every supporter of democracy is obliged to supply some sort of answer. Indeed the history of the democratic idea can be seen as a series of responses to the Socratic challenge. The important point here is that the Framers accepted much of the classical critique. They agreed that the generality of men tended to be foolish or worse. Moreover, the Framers did not need ancient writers to teach them the dangers. We have seen with what alarm and disapproval they regarded some of the things majorities had done in the states; for them, Shays' Rebellion was a frightening portent of what enraged masses might do. Thus it is easy to find quotations vividly demonstrating their fears regarding democracy. For example, in the 1787 Convention, Elbridge Gerry warned that "the evils we experience flow from the excess of democracy" [May 31], and Edmund Randolph complained of "the turbulence and follies of democracy" [May 31].

It must be granted, therefore, that the Framers wanted to get rid of democratic "excess" and "turbulence and follies." But did they do it by getting rid of democracy? The careless inference has been that the Framers—like most statesmen and writers until that time—rejected democracy as vicious or unworkable. But this misses the whole point of what distinguished the Framers from such predecessors. They agreed on democracy's weaknesses and dangerous tendencies, but they did not reject democracy. Indeed, they almost could not. They knew that whether they liked it or not they had to conform to the "popular genius" of American institutions. They accepted democracy and sought to guard against its "turbulence and follies." James Madison stated their view perfectly: They wanted to eliminate or lessen "the inconveniencies of democracy," but only in a manner "consistent with the democratic form of Government." Their candid appraisal of the faults to which democracy is prone must not obscure the central fact: They sought solutions *within a democratic framework*. This is the simple but vital truth in the old-fashioned view that the American constitutional system was "an experiment in democracy." The Framers wanted to "make *démocratie* safe for the world."[5]

What Democratic Government Is

But it does not settle the matter to say that the Framers intended a democratic form of government. We need ourselves to know what democracy is to judge whether the intention was fulfilled. Then we can judge whether separation of powers, for example, is in fact compatible with democracy and, if it is, how it nonetheless guards against democracy's "inconveniencies."

It is not easy to define democracy. To know what the democratic form of government is requires knowing what the other forms of government are. Unfortunately, distinguishing the forms or kinds of government is a central task of political science. It is the frustrating and fascinating fact that the beginning student of American government must grapple with the very difficulties that bedevil mature scholarship.

Who rules? Forms of government may best be distinguished according to two factors: who rules, and with what characteristic consequences, problems and weaknesses. Let us deal first with the factor of rule. The harsh fact is that the rule of some men over others is intrinsic to governing. Government is all about the question: What is to be done that will be binding upon the entire community? Conflicting answers arise and a decision must be made among them. Every form of government must therefore assign to some person or persons the final say, the authority to give the binding answer. That is what Tocqueville means in the passage quoted at the beginning of this chapter: "social power superior to all others must always be placed somewhere." He warns that, if liberty is to be preserved, this power's course must be retarded so it may have "time to moderate its own vehemence." As we shall see, this is exactly what the Constitution does. But as Tocqueville makes clear, to retard the course cannot mean failing to designate a final social power.

The "cracy" of the "demos." Who is and must be the final "social power" in the democratic form of government? The early use of the word democracy suggests the answer. Democracy is a word of Greek origin. There is little difficulty with the *cracy.* It derives from *kratein,* meaning to rule. However, a difficulty arises with *demo.* It derives from the Greek *demos* and is usually translated as the people. Thus democracy is usually said to have meant originally rule of or by the people. But that is, so to speak, a soft translation, obscuring the fact that rule means rule by some over others. As Plato and Aristotle, for example, used the term, the *demos* were not the whole people. Rather they thought that the 'people' included at least two groups—the *demos* and the *aristoi. Demos* meant the many. *Aristoi* meant the best. More fully, as the philosophers used the words, *aristoi* came to mean the few who are best. *Demos* came to mean the many who are not best; that is, the great majority of men who are poor, and thus uneducated (and perhaps uneducable), and thus unfit to rule well.

The vital point here is contained in the Greek philosophers' emphasis that democracy means the rule of the majority over everybody else, including any dissident minority. Democratic government necessarily operates by majority rule. Abraham Lincoln made the point with compelling logic in his First Inaugural Address: "Unanimity is impossible; the rule of a minority, as a permanent arrangement, is wholly inadmissible; so that, rejecting the majority principle, anarchy or despotism in some form is all that is left." In short, government 'by the people' means that the greater number of people rules the lesser. As Jefferson said in his First

Inaugural Address, "the will of the majority is in all cases to prevail."

The characteristics of majority rule. But there is more to democracy than merely numerical majority rule. Democracy's nature further consists in the characteristic problems that arise when the majority rules and in the characteristic ends for which the majority strives. Each form of government has peculiar strengths and weaknesses and peculiar ends or purposes. These differ with the differences in the personality, so to speak, of the rulers. In each form of government the ruling element tends to seek its own advantage, or to pursue the common good according to its own characteristic view of that good. Monarchs, aristocrats, and popular majorities tend to have very different ideas of what the national interest is and how to achieve it. Each regime is the bundle of behavior that results from this central fact.

A famous passage from Tocqueville on the propensities of democracy is an excellent example of reasoning in this manner:

> If you hold it expedient to divert the moral and intellectual activity of man to the production of comfort and the promotion of general well-being; . . . [if you] are content to meet with fewer noble deeds, provided offenses be diminished in the same proportion; if, instead of living in the midst of a brilliant society, you are contented to have prosperity around you; if, in short you are of the opinion that the principal object of a government is not to confer the greatest possible power and glory upon the body of the nation, but to ensure the greatest enjoyment and to avoid the most misery to each of the individuals who compose it—if such be your desire, then . . . establish democratic institutions.[6]

But the question of democracy's nature and propensities is a much disputed matter, and we cannot fully settle it here. For our purposes it is sufficient to define democratic government as that form which operates by majority rule and pursues the national interest in the manner characteristic of the majority. This was the way the Constitution's Framers regarded democracy. And, having accepted the democratic form, they set about guarding their system against the follies and evils democracies had hitherto exhibited. In their view, the typical folly to be avoided was the inability of the short-sighted majority to sustain a government and policies competent to serve the long-run national interest; and the typical evil was suppression by a tyrannical majority of the rights of minorities.

Democracy and liberty? *Democratic* suppression of *liberty?* Are democracy and liberty separable and indeed capable of opposing each other? This manner of viewing them is easy to derive from the Declaration's two principles—consent and rights. The Framers, and writers like Tocqueville, viewed the problem in this manner. They emphasize the majority rule aspect of democracy and its potential conflict with liberty. But many modern political scientists argue that liberty and democracy are inseparable and, therefore, that democracy, *by very definition*, includes liberty.[7] They grant that without majority rule there can be no democracy. But they insist that without liberty there can be no majority rule. The identity of the true majority and what it wants cannot be known until everybody has been freely heard from and a fair election held. In this view, democracy requires the continuous formation and reformation of majorities, a process that requires freedom of discussion and political organization.

The Framers and Tocqueville would reply: But of course *decent* democracy cherishes liberty; majorities must strive to respect liberty. However, to make liberty part of the very definition of democracy is to beg the key question: Are majorities *in fact* respecting the rights of others? For the sake of simplicity and clarity, in this book the idea of liberty is considered separately from the idea of democracy. Accordingly, we emphasize majority rule as the root of the democratic idea, the better to be able to see whether American majorities rule competently and with due regard to liberty.

Democracy or republic? But is America not a republic rather than a democracy? And weren't the Founding Fathers republicans rather than democrats?[8] The title of this book indicates our answers to these questions.

The single source most relied upon by those who make the republic-democracy distinction is *Federalist* 10. Countless references to the alleged radical distinction have been drawn from that essay. Ironically, *Federalist* 10 actually narrows the difference between the two terms and draws them more closely together than they had ever before been. It makes a republic simply a particular kind of democracy. The word republic comes from the Latin *respublica, res* meaning thing or affair, and *publica* meaning public as against private. For two thousand years, 'republic' usually simply meant any kind of nonmonarchical government; that is, any government in which politics was a public affair and not the personal prerogative of a king. Thus there were aristocratic republics, oligarchic republics, democratic republics, all kinds of republics. But Publius used the word to mean only a *democratic* republic.[9]

The modern confusion arises in part from neglecting to notice that *Federalist* 10 contrasts a republic with a *pure* democracy. That is, for Publius, republics differ not from democracy in general, but only from a pure democracy. For him a pure democracy is one in which "citizens . . . assemble and administer the government in person." A republic, he says, differs from this in only one way. It is "a government in which the scheme of representation takes place." Now this single difference is extremely important because, it is the basis of the Constitution's "cure" for democracy's "turbulence and follies." But for Publius a republic is simply a representative form of democracy. Accordingly, the best modern synonym for what the founding generation meant by republic is what Hamilton indeed called the new government—a "representative democracy."[10]

But this is not to depreciate the utility of the word republic. It has a valuable rhetorical ring. Unlike the word democracy, it conjures up worthy old-fashioned ideas of restraint and sobriety, of competence and liberty—that is, the very qualities democratic government needs to be its best self. Conservatives are therefore right in favoring the word, as they do; but they are wrong in thinking that the word republic of itself will somehow exorcise the social and economic policies that they detest. Whatever its rhetorical utility, it is impossible to read majority rule out of the American republic, as some have wished to do. This is confirmed by a simple verbal test. Suppose we say that America is a republic and not a democracy. Does not the question immediately arise: What kind of republic? And must the answer not be: a *democratic* republic?

In the very essay from which the radical distinction between republic and democracy has been drawn, Publius makes clear how very democratic the American republic is to be. He states bluntly that there is nothing that a determined, compact majority cannot constitutionally do.

> [A minority] will be unable to execute and mask its violence under the forms of the Constitution. [But] when a majority is included in a faction, the form of popular government . . . enables it to sacrifice to its ruling passion or interest both the public good and the rights of other citizens.

In short, in the American democratic republic—because it is democratic—the majority may commit its excesses *legally*, that is, "under the forms of the Constitution." The majority is the "final social power" designated by the Constitution. Appreciating the fullness of majority power under the Constitution is thus prerequisite to understanding the constitutional system. With that power acknowledged, we can proceed to consider how the system nonetheless guards liberty and supplies reasonably competent government.

THE EXTENDED REPUBLIC: "A MULTIPLICITY OF INTERESTS"

The cure for irresponsible majority power, *The Federalist* argued, lies above all in a potentiality of the representative principle: It makes possible an extended republic. Without representative institutions, democracy must confine itself to a small area; a representative democracy, however, may embrace a "greater number of citizens and greater sphere of country." This extension of number and sphere is the indispensable basis of the American constitutional design. To grasp this we must examine in detail James Madison's famous argument is that democratic remedies for the defects of democratic government are made possible in a very large republic.

> In the extended republic of the United States, and among the great variety of interests, parties, and sects which it embraces, a coalition of a majority of the whole society could seldom take place on any other principles than those of justice and the general good.[11]

What Size Makes Possible: "A Coalition of a Majority"

Note that nothing in the large republic solution prevents majorities from forming; that would be undemocratic and is thus excluded. Nor is the formation of factions in general discouraged, either by denying groups the freedom to organize or by reducing all men to an undifferentiated mass. On the contrary, the large republic engenders the formation of a very great number of factions. In turn this sheer multiplicity of factions will stifle the formation of the only majority to be feared, the one that would be adverse to "justice and the general good." Madison believed that, because it would be large enough, the American republic would have a great variety of groupings, no single one of which would comprise a majority of the people. Majorities would therefore have to form by coalition, a deliberate association of the smaller groups. The process of coalition would moderate these majorities so that free and competent government would result democratically from them. This concept of majority-by-coalition is crucial to Madison's theory and to the American political system which embodies it.

"The Most Common and Durable Sources of Factions"

What are these factions, coalitions of which form safe majorities? Madison knew that many forces separate men into conflicting factions. He knew that men divide over religious and political opinions, that they flock to rival ambitious leaders and that, when there is no serious divisive issue, "the most frivolous and fanciful distinctions" (perhaps like the struggle of Gulliver's Lilliputians over which end of a soft-boiled egg to open) may cause violent conflict.

> But the most common and durable source of factions has been the *various* and *unequal* distribution of property. Those who hold and those who are without property have ever formed distinct interests in society. Those who are creditors, and those who are debtors, fall under a like discrimination. A landed interest, a manufacturing interest, a mercantile interest, a moneyed interest, with many lesser interests, grow up of necessity in civilized nations, and divide them into different classes actuated by different sentiments and views [emphasis supplied].

Madison put the same thought another way: From "the possession of different *degrees* and *kinds* of property . . . ensues a division of the society into different interests and parties." [Emphasis supplied.] No pussy-footing here about economics as a prime factor in political conflict; the Framers believed that political conflict occurs most commonly and durably over economic interests. But notice that economic factors operate in two ways. Men possess "unequal" amounts or "degrees" of property and may divide accordingly. Or they can conflict over the "varieties" or "kinds" of property. The first way, division over amount of wealth, leads to the class struggles that destroyed so many older democracies—the mortal combat of the few rich against the many poor. Here is the key: Mortal class struggle is precisely what can be minimized or forestalled in the extended republic. There men will organize the second way, according to diversity in *kinds* of property. And conflict over *kinds* of property provides the context for free and competent democratic government.

Madison versus Marx. The contrast between the two forms of economic conflict is seen by contrasting Madison and Karl Marx. First, it should be clear from Madison's emphasis on economics that Karl Marx (1818-83) did not invent the idea that economics has something to do with politics, or even the idea that rich and poor tend to be natural political enemies. Indeed, all political thinkers knew that. Socrates said that within a city there are two cities "warring with each other, one of the poor, the other of the rich."[12] Similarly, the nineteenth-century Tory prime minister of England, Benjamin Disraeli, spoke of "The Two Nations."[13] Thus, Marxism must be seen more precisely, as a specific view of the economic factor. Marxism was based on an historical theory that the perennial rich-poor conflict was reaching a final climax in the advanced industrial nations. It was taking the final form of the capitalist-proletarian class struggle and would end with the triumph of the proletariat. Thus would be ushered in the socialist utopia, wherein the human condition itself would be transformed.

The key point is that Marxism depends upon the first sort of economic conflict—class conflict over inequality of amounts of property. Madison's strategy is precisely opposed; it seeks to subordinate this class conflict to the conflict between kinds of property. That is, in the extended republic the conflict of limited and specific interests replaces the divisive and general struggle between two great classes. In this sense, Madison anticipated and refuted Marxism. Rather than compacting into two distinct great classes, in Madison's theory, rich and poor are fragmented and jumbled together into narrow and particular "factions." Accordingly, no single owning class oppresses the masses; and the masses do not organize as a class, but rather fragment and factionally advance specialized, immediate interests.

This is just what has happened. One of the remarkable features of American politics is the absence of powerful Marxist movements like those in Western Europe. American trade unions have never been as influenced by socialism as their European counterparts. Friedrich Engels, Marx's great colleague, commented in 1892 on the unique absence of a major socialist party in America:

> There is no place yet in America for a *third* party, I believe. The divergence of interests even in the *same* class group is so great in that tremendous area that wholly different groups and interests are represented in each of the two big parties.[14]

There has been no such powerful third party since. The "divergence of interests . . . in that tremendous area" —Madison's theory of the extended republic—was built into the constitutional system. And that system has consistently operated, as he intended and as Engels noted, to help the American democracy avert the fatal politics of class struggle.

The Large Commercial Republic

Tremendous area does not of itself produce the divergence of interests of which Engels complained and upon which the constitutional system depends. We can see precisely what kind of large republic alone does that by analyzing the defect of small republics. The smaller the republic, "the fewer probably will be the distinct parties and interests composing it; the fewer the distinct parties and interests, the more frequently will a majority be found of the same party." The assumption is that small countries tend to have fewer interests because they have "small," relatively simple and undifferentiated economies.[15] This is an idea straight out of Adam Smith, who showed that a modern, highly differentiated economy depends upon a *large market area.* Mass markets make mass production possible. And mass production is highly specialized production—the division of labor into many specialized industries and specialized occupations and hence specialized interests. Thus, largeness is valuable because it makes possible the large *commercial* republic which proliferates economic interests. This proliferation is the variety of property which produces the moderate conflict upon which the constitutional system depends.

Let us sum up the utility of the extended commercial republic. The 'have-nots' (or 'have-lesses') everywhere outnumber the 'haves.' Democracy enables the have-not majority to vote themselves the wealth of the haves. This may go to such lengths as to cause mortal civil strife. One great task of the constitutional system is to prevent the "poor majority" and the "rich minority" from thinking of themselves as such and acting as such. This cannot be done in small countries with undifferentiated economies, where the mass of people are divided into but a few industries and occupations. These few differences seem trivial as compared with the great difference between all the poor, on one side, and all the rich on the other.[16] In a small republic, because the ways of being poor are so few, the mass unites in mortal combat with the rich, who similarly are compacted into a class because the ways of being rich are few and relatively noncompetitive. Only in the extended commercial republic can the mass be fragmented into a great variety of interests. When thus fragmented, men seek immediate gains for their particular industries or occupations and not the advantage of their class.

As an example of the process, consider only a single sector of the complex American economy—the transportation industry. There is in fact no single transportation industry. Instead there are the bus, truck, train, aircraft and maritime industries, each with dozens of subdivisions. And within each industry there are literally hundreds of specialized crafts and occupations. What pattern emerges? *Not* "transport magnates" ranged against the "transport proletariat." Railroad and truck owners compete very much more than they collaborate. Railroad unions and teamster unions bitterly compete with each other. True, unions and owners conflict *within* their industries, but they frequently close ranks against other industries. Thus railroad owners and railroad unions cooperate *against* cooperating truck owners and truck unions, each seeking preferential treatment from legislatures and administrative agencies. Even within this single sector of the economy there is no basic class division but rather a welter of conflicting interests. It is from thousands of such interests that the moderating "coalition of a majority" must be formed.

Prerequisites: Democracy and Prosperity

It can be inferred that two basic conditions are required if the moderating consequences of multiplicity are to result. First, the society must be profoundly democratic. As we have seen, a major aim of the extended republic is to prevent the formation of both desperate majorities and ruthless minorities. But if social class barriers prevent economic interest groups from making limited gains, what difference will economic differentiation make? No matter how diverse the economy, an undemocratic social and political structure negates the desired political effects of economic diversity. Germany was long a case in point—large, diverse, commercial, yet torn by bitter political warfare. The reason is simple: Germany was persistently undemocratic in decisive respects. Only when a country is genuinely democratic will the diverse economic interests adopt the moderate political views and methods of those who confidently seek immediate, limited advantage. The case of the Soviet Union is similarly instructive. It is surely as large and possessed of as many diverse interests and sects as anything Madison had in mind. Yet, for all its *social* and *economic* diversity, the Soviet Union lacks the *political* factors necessary to make the Madisonian scheme work: It lacks a legal-political structure that summons up the socioeconomic diversity and makes it politically significant. Without that structure, mere socioeconomic pluralism may be rendered a nullity and useless for liberty, as the case of the Soviet Union suggests.

Second, the society must have an economy that is relatively prosperous, has some give in it, and, perhaps, is growing. If total quantity of wealth is scanty or fixed, the distribution of wealth tends to become rigidly fixed on the existing class lines. Economic scarcity exacerbates the political struggle of the rich and poor. In a fixed and scanty economy, the poor have in practice little hope of improving their situation save by an assault upon the wealthy few. Accordingly, only a relatively prosperous economy, where patterns of distribution can easily change, encourages diverse economic groups to focus their energies on increasing their immediate share, rather than on politically fatal economic class warfare.

Religious Diversity: "the Multiplicity of Sects"

But even economic diversity plus democracy and prosperity, Madison observed, was not sufficient to secure the full range of liberties. He therefore also stressed a noneconomic aspect of the extended republic—religious diversity. He and the other leading Framers shared the eighteenth century's revulsion against religious fanaticism and tyranny. During the devastating religious struggles of the preceding two centuries, dominantly Catholic or Protestant governments had extinguished domestic liberties and warred with countries of the opposing creed. Other countries, where the two groups were more evenly divided, had been torn by bitter internal struggles. Madison saw in the extended republic a defense against such religiously provoked tyranny and domestic convulsion:

> In a free government the security for civil rights must be the same as that for religious rights. It consists in the one case in the multiplicity of interests, and in the other in the multiplicity of sects. The degree of security in both cases will depend on the number of interests and sects; and this may be presumed to depend on the extent of country and number of people comprehended under the same government.[17]

He argued that, so strong was the human propensity to religious domination, only sectarian fragmentation would effectively prevent waves of fanaticism from sweeping across a nation. This fragmentation or multiplicity is likelier in extended republics, as was clear in the case of America. (Consider the greater likelihood of religious dominance and conflict had America broken into several independent nations; a single sect might well have emerged as a domineering majority in each.) Religious multiplicity is thus immensely important in the American polity. Since no single sect can by itself achieve a national majority, religious multiplicity necessitates the moderating process of coalition, which in turn offers all religious sects ultimate national protection against oppressive local majorities. In all of this, Madison was following the penetrating views of the eighteenth century French philosopher, Voltaire. "If there were only one religion in England, despotism would have to be feared; if there were two, they would cut each other's throats; but they have thirty, and they live happily and in peace."[18]

Representation and the Process of Coalition

The representative principle makes the extended republic and its multiplicity possible. Moreover, it is at the level of the representative that much of the moderating process of coalition occurs. As the spokesman for the interest groups dominant in his state or district, the representative may be loyally prepared to sacrifice the national interest to their extreme demands. But he and those he represents soon learn that they simply do not have the votes. In order to secure congressional majorities for desired legislation or to win the presidency, cooperation with other groups proves necessary. Thus ensues the coalescing process. As the coalition enlarges to form the necessary majority, an enormous number of conflicting selfish interests must be taken in account. The groups within the emerging coalition must at least make concessions to each other's needs. In the process, the grossest demands of each tend to be moderated. It becomes difficult to formulate laws and policies favoring the coalition members that are not at the same time roughly compatible with "justice and the general good."

Thus, even in terms of the narrowest selfishness, multiplicity and the coalition process tend to moderate the worst effects of that selfishness. But something more valuable than that can happen. The discovery that one's grossest demands are absurdly impossible of achievement can lead to an enlightened kind of self-interest, a habitual recognition of the indisputable needs of others and a sobriety about the general requirements of society. And something still worthier can happen. As the extremes of selfishness are moderated, the representative can become free to consider questions affecting the national interest on their merits. The jostling of innumerable interests gives him a margin of freedom from any single interest group. He is thereby enabled, to some extent, to pursue the national interest as he comes to see it in the instructive national arena.

> The aim of every political constitution is, or ought to be, first to obtain for rulers men who possess most wisdom to discern, and most virtue to pursue, the common good of the society; and in the next place, to take the most effectual precautions for keeping them virtuous whilst they continue to hold their public trust.[19]

REPRESENTATIVE GOVERNMENT

A major problem in the American Republic, therefore, is the democratic choice of this wisdom and virtue—democratic choice because the whole system rests upon choice by majority rule; wise and virtuous representatives because of the republican belief that government of and for the people more competently solves problems and protects liberties when it is conducted by such representatives rather than by the people themselves. The representative is thus viewed as more than a mere mouthpiece for his electors. The presumption is that the representatives will be able men who, in congress assembled, will deliberate and judge wisely on behalf of the people. Ultimately the quality of the representatives—legislative, executive and judicial—depends upon the decency and sense of the electorate. No constitution can indefinitely protect a vicious or foolish people. But the constitutional arrangements (and the moral tone of a constitution) can increase the likelihood that citizens will choose capable men. The Constitution conduces to the choice of such representatives in three main ways: by the nature of the public offices; by the size and variety of the electoral district; and by indirect election and appointment.

Constitutional Bases of Capable Representation

The nature of the offices: Men of the requisite capacity seek office only when the office offers opportunities adequate to their abilities and ambitions. The Constitution creates such national offices—independent, powerful, honorific, and of sufficient duration. Precisely because national office constitutionally affords great power and honor, able and ambitious men can pursue political careers within the constitutional framework rather than by unconstitutional adventurism. Nor does all of this assume that thirst for high office is merely a lust for power. Rather, as modern corporation executives, for example, tell us, the ablest men gravitate to posts where authority is sufficient for accomplishing great tasks. Further, the terms of the national offices are constitutionally fixed, preventing arbitrary removal, and are of sufficient duration to attract able men. The 4-

year president, 6-year senators, and life-tenure judges have sufficient time to pursue long-range plans. The possibility of reelection increases the prospective time. (The Twenty-second Amendment, which limits presidents to two terms, departs radically from this original constitutional principle.) Finally, Congress sets the pay for national offices. National compensation has usually been sufficient for almost anyone to try a political career, and it has usually been higher than that of comparable office in most Western European countries.

The size and variety of electoral districts to be represented in an extended republic: Since the number of offices does not increase proportionally with the size of the republic, each district tends to possess a "greater number of citizens and extent of territory." Further, the more complex and varied the national economy, the more each large district is likely to reproduce the valuable multiplicity. Thus not only presidents and senators but even representatives are elected from districts where the multiplicity-coalition process is at work. Consequently, candidates must appeal to diverse interests and win wide popular support. The ability to win such an election inclines[20] the successful candidate toward the decent and moderate quality of representation which the system requires. Moreover, representatives from such districts need not be the captive of any one group but rather can find some elbow-room for statesmanship in the very confusion of factions.

The partial constitutional reliance on *indirect election* and *appointment:* In the original Constitution, the House of Representatives was the only directly elected branch. But the word "only" is misleading: the "only" directly elected branch was also the most powerful branch. In a system based on legislative supremacy, the directly popular House was expected to be the most authoritative organ of government. However, the Senate was to be indirectly elected (also the President, but for different reasons), and the judges were to be appointed. So long as the system was based squarely on the directly popular House, James Madison favored this "policy of refining the popular appointments by successive filtrations."[21] He agreed that men chosen by the people could in turn choose better qualified senators and judges. The Seventeenth Amendment (1913) has since further democratized the Constitution by requiring direct popular election of the Senate. The original constitutional preference for an appointive judiciary has, however, remained unchanged. Unlike many state judiciaries which are elective, the entire national judiciary is appointive.

Representation and Majority Rule

The Constitution, then, encourages merit in government by means of the nature of the offices, size of constituencies, and mode of election or appointment. But is the very idea of encouraging merit compatible with democracy? The answer must be Yes, unless one believes that democracy must mean rule by random numbers or, worse, rule by the least fit.[22] The relevant question then is: Are these constitutional means compatible with the idea of democratic representation? For example, granted that fixed terms and great powers of office help make government competent, is it democratic to give men powerful office for two, four, or six years or for life in the case of the judiciary? Perhaps it would be more democratic if the people could change the government whenever they wished, or decide important governmental matters by weekly referenda. Or would that really be more democratic? In such confusion and chaos, would not machine politicians or hidden wire-pullers or demagogues in fact become the real rulers? "The countenance of the government may become more democratic, but the soul that animates it will be more oligarchic."[23] In short, a, seemingly purer, democratic system might become one in name only. In contrast, American government in practice is extremely responsive to popular pressure. Members of the House of Representatives are kept on a very short two-year tether; and, although Senators have a six-year term, one-third of the Senate is elected every two years. Presidents painfully learn how much a 'mid-term' Congress can change their political landscape. Not only relatively frequent elections (and the anticipation of them) keep Congress and President democratically responsive; the whole political process of interest group activity and of the mass media of communication presses down upon them, keeping them constantly aware of changing group demands and shifts in public opinion.

But how about indirect election of the Senate and the President and judicial appointment? These have often wrongly been attributed to the Framers' alleged radical distrust of the electorate. Reflection reveals that a determined and sustained majority, from the outset, has always been able constitutionally to impose its will despite indirect election and appointment. In order to understand their relationship to the democratic principle, Senate, President and judges must each be considered separately.

First, the indirect selection of the Senate by the state legislatures was in part simply a compromise on the federal-national question; it was a concession to the 'pure federalists' who wanted the states as such to have a place in the electoral process. Further, the Framers were faced with the task of differentiating the Senate from the House. In constructing their bicameral legislature (see pp. 95 ff.), they had abandoned the aristocratic features that characterized all traditional second chambers like the English House of Lords; thus they considered indirect election a way of distinguishing the Senate from the House that would not violate republican principles. (Interestingly, there was very little contemporary criticism of the Senate as undemocratic on the grounds that it was indirectly elected.) Finally, consider that the state legislatures which were to appoint the Senate were themselves remarkably democratic bodies close to popular opinion. Contests for election to the state legislature frequently became in effect popular contests over rival candidates for the Senate. Besides, as early as 1800, candidates for state legislatures typically were identified with political parties. Thus, in voting for the legislative candidate, the citizen knew that he was choosing between two parties and, therefore, between the rival senatorial favorites of the two parties. Indirect election was undoubtedly less purely democratic than direct election. But more often than not popular opinion prevailed; the method was not decisively undemocratic in intention or consequences.

The indirect election of the President has an entirely different genesis from the initially indirect election of the Senate. It is a mistake to think that the Framers pondered whether to elect the President directly or indirectly. The real question at the Convention was whether to have the President chosen by the people, by the states, or by the national legislature. On that issue, the Convention decided overwhelmingly. They rejected election by states—legislatures or executives—to keep him independent of state domination; for the same reason, independence, they chose not to have him elected by the national legislature. The decision was emphatically to have a popular, nationwide choice of the President. Once this was decided, the real problem became how it could be accomplished in practice. The Framers sought to avoid giving opportunities for foreign and domestic intrigue around this important choice; and they feared that the primitive state of national communications would make it impossible for the people of one state to know the first citizens of another. The device of an electoral college (electors had already been used with success in some states) as an *ad hoc* body constituted only for the purposes at hand, meeting in thirteen different states, made the first occurrence unlikely. The requirement that each elector vote for two candidates, at least one of whom had to be from a state other than his own, overcame the second difficulty until such time as nationhood made it more likely that prominent citizens would be generally known. Indirect election almost immediately became subject to an additional popular control (as was the case with the senatorial election). As Jefferson wrote in 1816, election via the Electoral College was nonetheless "election by the people, in *practice* (for they vote for [elector] A only on an assurance he will vote for [candidate] B.)."[24] Nothing in the Constitution impeded this development. On the contrary, the Framers created a national, popularly elective Presidency with the best means available; and with means wholly open to further democratic development.[25]

The nonelective character of the national judiciary—the fact that Supreme Court justices are appointed by the President with the "advice and consent of the Senate"—has been little criticized. And yet on its face, especially considering judicial life tenure, this mode of appointment is less democratic than the popular election of judges. But the Framers have not been faulted as antidemocrats because the reasons for the appointive mode are so manifestly sensible. That is, the Framers obviously did not choose the appointive mode in order to evade the democratic principle. Rather, there was nearly universal agreement that this was the best way to secure the peculiar qualifications necessary to an independent judiciary. In most moderate governments—democratic, aristocratic or monarchic —efforts are made to appoint and organize the judiciary so as to secure its independence. Moreover, a democratic safeguard was built into the appointive process. The President's judicial nominees must face the scrutiny of the Senate. Although the Senate has rarely rejected a Court appointee, the possibility of such rejection is a constant constraint on the Executive: In 1968 one of the rare rejections occurred. When President Johnson nominated Justice Abe Fortas to be Chief Justice, intense senatorial criticism caused Justice Fortas to remove himself from consideration.

Granted then that the Constitutional arrangements are formally compatible with democracy, or that determined majorities can constitutionally overcome these specific 'retarding' obstacles. But are there hidden barriers to democracy? A representative system may be made undemocratic either by suffrage qualifications (limiting voters) or by representative qualifications limiting those who may be elected) . . . [The main conclusions on the suffrage question are:] There was a very broad electorate in 1787; it was expected to broaden steadily; it was sufficiently broad to be deemed a democratic suffrage then and has broadened steadily since. As to qualifications upon the representatives, "no qualification of wealth, of birth, of religious faith, or of civil profession is permitted to fetter the judgment or disappoint the inclination of the people."[26] The national system totally excluded undemocratic qualifications although these lingered on in some states. Regardless of origin or previous condition, anyone could aspire to national office. This legal fact immediately and profoundly democratized the political process. Finally, note the relatively generous provisions admitting citizens of foreign origin to public office in a country where immigration reached unprecedented proportions. No hidden barrier here to the influence of the newly arriving immigrants.

The constitutional system of representation is thus thoroughly compatible with "the spirit and the form of popular government." Yet to demonstrate the legal power of majorities under the Constitution is not to suggest that a tyrannically-minded majority can readily overcome the "retarding" obstacles. Nor does it suggest that it should. But to appreciate the restraining constitutional devices is to understand that sustained majorities *can* rule under the forms of the Constitution. It is to these forms or devices that we now turn.

SEPARATION OF POWERS

Separation of the legislative, executive, and judicial powers of government into separate branches of government is the fundamental institutional feature of the national government.[27] Two familiar ideas underlie the concept of separation of powers:

> The accumulation of all powers, legislative, executive, and judiciary, in the same hands, whether of one, a few, or many and whether hereditary, self-appointed, or elective, may justly be pronounced the very definition of tyranny. . . . [T]he preservation of liberty requires that the three great departments of power should be separate. . . .[28]

First, the mere "accumulation" or concentration of power is deemed tantamount to tyranny because any such monopoly of power will inevitably be abused. Second, salvation lies in distributing power among three branches of government. All this seems so familiar and natural that Americans cannot imagine sensible men looking at the matter in any other light. But the separation of powers was still a novel idea when the American system was created and it is not universally accepted today.

It is indeed natural to analyze governing into its component parts, but the separation of powers theory is only one particular way of making the analysis. For example, Aristotle's *Politics* does not use the legislative executive-judicial trio, but rather sees the component parts as the *deliberative,* the part of the *magistrates,* and the part of the *judges.* The "deliberative" is a very broad category including the most important judicial tasks and many tasks we now think of as executive. Moreover, Aristotle does not distribute these 'functions' according to their nature to separate branches of government. For example, deliberation may be divided between the magistrates and the assembly, with the most important tasks often being assigned to the magistrates. According to Aristotle, then, who does what is not settled simply by the nature of the function, but rather should vary from regime to regime, depending on how the best governing can be gotten in the circumstances. This subtle view prevailed among philosophic writers for two thousand years; but in most countries, the various functions were not distributed according to any clear principle. A king, an aristocratic body, or popular assembly singly performed all the functions, or else they were haphazardly and overlappingly performed by various organs of government.

The separation of powers theory, developed by seventeenth and eighteenth century English publicists and by philosophers like Locke and Montesquieu, departed from Aristotle in two major ways. First, a new scheme of functions was developed: legislative-executive-judicial. Notice especially that Aristotle's 'deliberative' category is replaced by 'law-making' as the supreme political function. The importance of the change lies in this: Law is a narrower function than deliberation. Deliberation implies flexibility; it permits prudential discretion to rulers in dealing with particular problems. Law-making implies limitations and constraints; it tends to require that government follow set procedures and deal primarily with general rules rather than particular policies. That is, the idea of law-making as the supreme function points to limited government in which liberty is the highest aim.

Moreover, the separation of powers departed from the Aristotelian view in a second major way, involving the distribution of the functions. The new idea was that the difference in functions should become the principle of the governmental structure. That is, the three functions should systematically be distributed according to their nature among three branches; each function was to have its own branch of government. These are the two novel and striking features of the separation of powers.[29]

A Barrier to Tyranny over the People

In America, where the theory was subtly elaborated, the separation of powers has three aims, two dealing with tyranny and one with achieving competent government. The simplest of the three aims is to protect the people from tyrannical government. The idea is that power divided is power less likely to be used oppressively. In a more elegant eighteenth-century phrase—popular liberty is better secured when three distinct bodies must concur in schemes of usurpation and perfidy. The separate functions are thus entrusted to separate branches so that such perfidious concurrence is made less likely. The tyrannical tendency of any branch can be restrained by the resistance of the other two. For example, if a tyrannical law is passed, the executive and judiciary can mitigate its severity in the way they administer and apply it.

But the Framers knew that it was not enough to enshrine separation of powers merely in the parchment provisions of the Constitution. The danger was that one branch might in reality overwhelm the others and concentrate all power within itself, behind the facade of the Constitution. Accordingly, for separation of powers to be a barrier to tyranny, it must neutralize not governmental tyranny in general, but tyranny in the various forms it can take—legislative, executive, or judicial tyrannies in particular.

Danger from the executive branch. Was executive tyranny the chief fear? Did not the Declaration of Independence strike the basic and permanent note when it tied American independence to a struggle against executive tyranny in the person of King George III? Yet the leading Framers had reasons for not regarding the executive as the greatest danger in the new system. On the contrary, they thought that the outstanding lesson of the post-Revolutionary decade was the tendency to executive feebleness.

The legislatures, they believed, had become dangerously dominant in the new state governments; they believed also that this legislative predominance was the natural tendency of representative democracies. And, of course, the Articles of Confederation, for 'pure federal' reasons, had necessarily lacked a strong national executive. Thus, far from being concerned to hamstring the executive, the Framers wanted to create a strong executive branch, confident that the other elements of the constitutional system would sufficiently guard against executive tyranny over the people.

Their confidence rested upon two main checks provided by the system, as well as upon the separation of powers. First, the Presidency is basically a democratic elective office; the people can vote a dangerous President out of office. The citizenry from the outset, despite indirect election by the Electoral College, decisively influenced the outcome. Presidential power, like all political power under the Constitution, results primarily from winning majorities in free, popular elections. Second, although a very powerful office, the executive still lacks one supremely dangerous ingredient—the prerogative. This was the British king's area of personal and independent authority, a vast region of little-defined discretionary power, relatively free from parliamentary control, the king's to exercise as he desired; it was thus always a threat in the background to constitutional government. The President is constitutionally vested with the very broad executive power and thus has in truth a "touch of the prerogative." But his powers must derive from the Constitution; he can not readily appeal to any source, like the prerogative, beyond it. (E.g., he cannot, as the executive can in many countries, independently declare a national emergency and suspend "the ordinary processes of government.")

Of course, the separation of powers itself profoundly restrains the Presidency. The bulk of governing powers is constitutionally granted to a Congress; and the senators and representatives—close to popular opinion, closely allied with local interest groups, rooted in state politics, and vividly aware of their legislative dignities—are a strong check upon the executive. Finally, the President has to deal with a powerful and independent judiciary which has asserted broad authority to set boundaries and give meanings to the laws he enforces and to his means of enforcing them.

These restraints, which made the leading Framers little fearful of executive tyranny, have worked. Election, limited discretionary power, and the necessity for more or less peaceful coexistence with Congress and the courts result in an executive safely kept—thus far at least—from tyrannizing over the people.

Danger from the legislative branch. What the constitutional designers really feared was legislative dominance. The representative legislature is the very essence of the democratic republican idea. Possessing most of the great powers of government and intimately connected with the interests and opinions of local constituencies, the lawmaking body was thought to have the advantage in conflicts with the other branches. The Framers regarded it as the branch likeliest to succeed in deceiving and dominating the people; this was the "elective despotism" Jefferson warned of. The Constitution's main institutional protection against the danger of legislative tyranny is the separation of powers. Because of the separation, the legislative needs the concurrence of the other two branches before its laws become effective; and the executive and judiciary, as we shall see, are given additional means to resist it. Further, the executive and judiciary can alert the people to the danger and rally them against any usurping movement in the legislative branch. The constitutional design thus depends on an executive and judiciary capable of combatting the legislature.

Danger from the Majority Itself

Thus far we have considered only the first aim of the separation of powers—preventing tyranny *over* the people, from whatever branch the tyranny originates. But it has a second and subtler aim. It seeks also to thwart tyranny *by* the people, that is, tyranny of the majority over minorities. Nothing in the structure of unseparated democratic governments slows down majority action; whatever Demos wants, Demos promptly gets. The separation of powers seeks to introduce a retarding factor. But separation of powers obstructs a tyrannizing majority differently and more subtly than it obstructs tyranny by government over the people. Against the latter, separation of powers relies upon and cooperates with majority rule. That is, the majority can rally behind a befriending branch or branches and in time can subdue the tyrannical branch. The problem is obviously different when the tyranny is supported by the majority itself. The legislative branch, for the same sort of reasons that it was deemed likeliest to tyrannize over the people, was deemed likeliest also to become the vehicle for tyranny by the majority. As a brake on majority tyranny, as we shall see, the aim of separation of powers is to create an executive and judiciary capable of temporarily blocking popular will as expressed through a compliant or demagogic legislature.

The Separation of Powers and Competent Government?

But the separation of powers does not function solely to forestall tyranny, whether over or by the people. That is how it is usually conceived. Indeed, many modern observers believe that the Framers were so excessively fearful of political power that they dangerously weakened and fragmented the government; that they set the separate branches against each other and thus encouraged stalemate and inefficiency—potentially disastrous in the modern world. But, ironically, this was not at all how the leading Framers understood what they were doing. On the contrary, they saw a third aim of separation of powers: It was the only practicable way then to strengthen government in general and assure some substantial coherence and effectiveness.

The modern critics blame stalemate on the ability of the separated Congress to frustrate presidential leadership. They contrast the 'obstructive' American Congress with the legislative body in an idealized parliamentary system where there is no separation of powers. There the executive is drawn from the legislature and functions within it with the support of tractable party majorities. The modern critics suggest that something like this would have provided stronger, more effective government in America.

But what kind of parliamentary system would in fact have been created in 1787? The best guess is one with the kind of weak executive then typical in the states and, moreover, one in which the centrifugal tendencies of American federalism would have had dangerously free play. Added to the tendency to executive feebleness in a representative democracy, the divisiveness of the states would probably have been fatal to any American parliamentary system. These divisive tendencies, so crippling under the Confederation, would probably have produced a Congress unwilling to create the strong executive a parliamentary system needs. (The same would probably be true today. Would the proud and suspicious states really be willing to submerge their identities in an all-powerful Parliament?) By contrast, under the Constitution the separate executive served from the outset as an integrating and nationalizing force. In any event, this was what the leading Framers wanted. They saw separation of powers not as a way to create a legislature capable of resisting the executive, but just the other way around. Accordingly, by virtue of separation of powers, the Constitution makes possible an independent and powerful executive, capable of curbing legislative anarchy or tyranny and of supplying leadership to the American polity.

Branches Capable of Retarding and Leading

In the American democratic republic there is no problem that Congress will not be a powerful and assertive body. That is easily provided for. But precisely how does the constitutional system provide an executive and judiciary capable of retarding threats to liberty from either the legislature or the people and of supplying long-range leadership? The first step is obvious: The executive and judiciary must be independent branches of government. Accordingly, the Constitution itself establishes as firmly as possible their jurisdictions, appointment processes, and financial bases; these matters are not left to the mercy of the legislature. But much more is required even than this.

The "mixture" of powers. Further, to give the executive the constitutional wherewithal to retard and lead, the Constitution partially *mixes* or *blends* as well as separates the powers of government. It does not treat each function of government as having exact boundaries, with each branch assigned exclusive jurisdiction over all aspects of its function. On the contrary, the executive is constitutionally assigned a *share* in the legislative power.[30] For example, the President's veto gives him, so to speak, one sixth of the legislative power. That is, it takes one sixth more (the difference between an ordinary and a two-thirds majority) of the vote of each house to override his veto. The President is also empowered, indeed required, to propose legislation and report to Congress on the "state of the Union." That is, he is constitutionally obliged to spend part of his time thinking as a legislator. Most legislation now is executive-originated and rests upon this constitutional base. (As to the judiciary, the judges have come to touch on the legislative realm quite specifically in reviewing the constitutionality of laws and other official acts, and they have a broad range of discretion in interpreting and applying the laws Congress makes.) One aim of this *mixture* of powers, paradoxically, is to achieve the maximum *separation* of powers practicable. The belief here is that the executive can maintain its independence of the popular legislature only when it is strengthened by sharing in the legislative power.

The "personal motives" to retard and lead. Checks upon power, however, are not automatically and invariably good things. Thus the doctrine of separation of powers does not intend that the branches should constantly obstruct each other. That would bring government, imbecilically, to a halt. Similarly, it is senseless if the separate branches prevent each other from acting justly or usefully. In short, the separation of powers makes sense only if it restrains what should be restrained while permitting efficient government otherwise. It makes sense, for example, *only* if presidents and judges typically restrain not majorities, but only *foolish* or *tyranni-cal* majorities. This is precisely the belief upon which the leading Framers acted: Separation would tend to forestall foolish and tyran-nical measures, while the separate branches would ordinarily col-laborate efficiently in proper measures.

A famous passage from *The Federalist* states the underlying argument:

> The great society . . . consists in giving to those who administer each department the necessary constitutional means and personal motives to resist encroachments of the others. . . . Ambition must be made to counteract ambition. The interest of the man must be connected with the constitutional rights of the place. . . . This policy of supplying, by opposite and rival interests, the defect of better motives, might be traced through the whole system of human affairs, private as well as public.[31]

Thus, the separation of powers must also mix the powers sufficiently so that each branch can resist the encroachments of the others, and especially so that presidents and judges will have the "constitutional means" to resist legislative encroachment. Notice: *constitutional* means. That is, only a regular, constitutional path is marked out; usurpation and subversion are neither necessary nor permitted. Once these means are exhausted, the business of governing proceeds.

But it is not enough, the argument runs, to equip the executive and judicial branches with the constitutional means to check the democratic legislature. They must also have the motives, that is, the will to resist and lead popular opinion. But why in a democratic society will they too not pander to popular favor? The answer is *not* that presidents and judges would always be men of outstanding virtue and wisdom. Rather, the constitutional system relies heavily on their "*personal* motives": The private passions and interests of presidents and judges are expected to lead them to protect liberty and advance long-run national interests; that is, to resist the democratic legislature when it factionally jeopardizes liberty and competent government, and to collaborate with it in all decent measures.

But what personal motives will perform this remarkable task? Only a very long excursion into political philosophy would lead to the answer. But the enigmatic passage just quoted supplies the main clue in the word ambition. Truly ambitious men do not readily yield to *momentary* popular clamor because thus yielding produces little *lasting* fame or power. Ambitious presidents and judges know that the dignity and privileges of their offices will be diminished in the long run if they make themselves mere puppets of the legislature and popular opinion. They will not want these offices made foolish or servile. The constitutional belief is that presidents and judges will stand firm for reasons of self-interest. They will gamble that their own power and prestige will be greater than ever when the majority comes to its senses. In this way, separation of powers seeks to supply democracy with officers who, because they hold important and powerful offices and because they can satisfy their ambitions in those offices, will tend to oppose momentary follies and self-destructive errors on the part of the democracy.

But the system does not depend entirely upon selfish personal interest. It relies also on the sense and decency of the office-holder and seeks to enhance that sense and decency. The executive and judiciary, as we have seen, are great offices, are based upon the broadest national constituency, are given tasks where the national interest most vividly presents itself, and are given terms of office sufficient to kindle their best ambitions. Under such circumstances they are expected to strive to be as big and national as the offices they hold, and to execute and adjudicate in the national interest skillfully, as it were, out of a sense of professional honor. Indeed, the constitutional system depends generally upon a certain portion of decency in the citizenry and their representatives. No constitutional scheme can indefinitely save a corrupt or utterly foolish people from disaster or tyranny. The Constitution presupposes a citizenry that appreciates liberty and is capable of pursuing its self-interest in an enlightened way. And it assumes an equal or greater portion of decency in the three branches of government, and that they will ordinarily cooperate efficiently under a properly arranged Constitution.

In short, the separation of powers is a rather fragile device, requiring good sense and moderation. The public generally, and presidents, judges, and legislators in particular, must respect the separate jurisdictions of the branches despite, indeed because of, the difficulty of drawing boundary lines. It must also be remembered that separation of powers is an organic part of a subtle constitutional system, needing other parts of the system for its own operation and itself in turn necessary to their functioning. For example, as we shall see, separation of powers is closely linked to bicameralism. Similarly, separation of powers depends upon the multiplicity of interests which lessens the likelihood of majority factions. (Of what use would separation of powers be if a determined Communist majority formed in this country? Would a Communist President, Communist Court, and Communist Congress check and balance each other?) At the same time, the very existence of the independent branches tends to foster the necessary multiplicity. The forming and reforming of diverse groups for immediate, limited purposes is encouraged by the differences in times and manner of election, sizes of constituencies, and kinds of power that characterize separation of powers.

BICAMERALISM

Bicameralism (from the Latin *bi*, meaning two, and *camera*, meaning a chamber) is the division of the legislature into two houses. It may be understood essentially as a variant of separation of powers. This suggests that there is more to bicameralism than the familiar opinion that Congress was divided simply so that the states might be equally represented in one house. Bicameralism is not limited to federal systems; it is also appropriate and is used in unitary systems. Indeed, the American Senate was organized as a separate house primarily for a guiding and restraining purpose entirely unconnected with federalism. Its origins suggest that purpose.

Precursors of Bicameralism

The American Senate can be understood in contrast with the ancient Roman Senate, the remote forebear from which it takes its name. The Roman Senate (from *senex*, meaning old and, presumably, wise) was supposed to counterbalance the popular will as expressed through other governing organs. In practice, the Roman Senate was selected by the aristocratic patricians; that is, it represented a social and economic class. The second house in the English system, the Lords, functioned similarly; it was an hereditary noble body counterbalancing the commoners. Medieval France had what could be called a tricameral system, consisting of the three estates (from the Latin *status*); the different bodies represented distinct classes within the society. These three earlier systems all presupposed aristocratic society, a society radically divided into different classes or stations in life. The divided legislative bodies were to represent these different classes in the society. Early bicameralism, if it can be called that, was thus part of the ancient idea of the mixed regime. This was the theory that the best practical government was one that blended the three pure forms of monarchy, aristocracy, and democracy. A king would superintend the general interests of society, separate bodies would represent the aristocracy and the general citizenry, and all three would be checks upon each other. The mixture was supposed to yield the best and avoid the worst aspects of each pure form.

Modern Democratic Bicameralism

The American version of bicameralism is fundamentally different because the American society is overwhelmingly democratic. The American Senate does not and cannot have the aristocratic foundation of the roughly comparable bodies in the earlier systems. It is designed to fit into a democratic system that rests upon ultimate majority rule. But the contrast with the earlier systems reveals a distinctive feature of the American Senate. The constitutional scheme is that, within a democratic polity, the Senate is in some ways to be the upper house, supplying some of the advantages of the old mixed regime idea. Rather like the separate executive and judiciary, the Senate is devised to prevent the excesses of the popular house:

> When the people . . . call for measures which they themselves will afterward . . . lament and condemn . . . how salutary will be the interference of some temperate and respectable body of citizens . . . to check . . . the blow meditated by the people against themselves, until reason, justice, and truth can regain their authority over the public mind.[32]

As the most directly popular organ of the government, the House has to be a large and, potentially, frequently changing body. But this, it was reasoned, makes it subject to erratic and ill-considered gusts in popular opinion. This, then, was the problem which had to be solved, but in a manner consistent with popular sovereignty. It is essential to understand that the key structural device of the Framers' solution to the perennial problem of democratic governments was the Senate: democratic bicameralism.[33] Madison, describing for Jefferson the results of the work of the Convention, referred to the Senate as "the great anchor of the Government."[34]

Accordingly, the Senate is made a much smaller body with greater continuity, the better to be able to check the presumably rash House, and to supply positive leadership as well. Competent government, especially in matters of foreign policy, requires system, long-range planning of "well-chosen and well-connected measures."[35] The popular House is less likely to supply such legislative leadership because its members serve shorter terms, are more often removed from office, and are more likely to be neglectful of national and long-run interests in favor of the wishes of the constituents they face every two years. The Senate is constructed to secure experience, stability, and a national outlook. Senators ordinarily come from large and hence more diversified constituencies. Their six-year term gives greater time for statesmanship. The system of staggered elections, by which only one third of the Senate can change during a given election, encourages continuity of policy. Further, the Senate is given greater responsibility than the House in the sobering areas of foreign affairs, appointing national officers, and judging impeachments.

Constitutionalism:
The Question of Limited Government

Constitutionalism is ordinarily understood as the opposite of unlimited and arbitrary political power. The aim of any constitution is indeed somehow to limit government so that rulers may not arbitrarily do whatever they please, whenever and however they please. But precisely what should be limited and by what means? No one limits anything merely for the sake of limitation. The question is always the *reason* for the limitations, that is, the ends that the limitations are intended to protect. (The American Constitution, for example, begins with a Preamble that states the ends for which the government is instituted.) Therefore the question of constitutionalism is always basically a question about the proper ends of government. The task of a constitution is to establish and maintain a government that pursues the particular ends wanted of it. Accordingly, theories of constitutionalism and actual constitutions differ largely according to the ends deemed proper for government to achieve.

The question of constitutionalism, then, involves the deepest of all political questions: For what purposes ought government to exist? What are its proper ends? What is proper political authority? One fundamental way in which all political thinkers deal with such questions is by distinguishing between arbitrary power and proper political authority. For example, Aristotle distinguishes between *healthy* and *perverted* constitutions or regimes, and Locke distinguishes between *legitimate* and *illegitimate* political power. Their difference is no trivial semantical matter. Rather, each has a profoundly different view of what government ought to do, from which it follows that each conceives of constitutionalism differently. Aristotle, emphasizing the ethical health or excellence of a regime, assigns to a constitution far more positive tasks than Locke, whose view of legitimate authority greatly limits the tasks of government.

We may understand Aristotle's view by considering the root of the word 'constitution.' It derives from the Latin *statuere* which means to 'set up' in the sense of giving a thing its essential and peculiar nature. But a thing does not acquire its fundamental nature merely because of negative limitations, but also because of positive things. In the ancient tradition, a constitution establishes the fundamental nature or genius of a political system; that is, a constitution is a people's peculiar way of life. Thus it consists in the human ends towards which a particular system strives, both by virtue of its positive arrangements as well as by virtue of limits placed upon its rulers. Consider how a people's way of life is positively determined by such constitutional arrangements as the composition of the electorate, the distribution of public offices, the behaviors it encourages or discourages. Accordingly, a constitution can encourage either commerce or agriculture, it can degrade the poor and make the wealthy arrogant or ameliorate poverty and blur class distinctions, it can make a people martial or pacific, it can require public piety and support for religion or separate church and state. And in these ways it shapes the very being of the society and forms the kinds of human beings who live in it.

In this old broad sense of the term, a constitution is clearly the most important of all influences upon political behavior. As we shall see, the American Constitution emphasizes the limiting aspect of constitutionalism; nonetheless it is impossible to understand American society without seeing the formative influence of the Constitution upon it. This book throughout emphasizes the influence upon political behavior of the formal constitutional arrangements and their intent.

Since the seventeenth century, the traditional view stressing both the positive and negative aspects of constitutionalism has given way to an emphasis on the negative or limiting aspect of constitutionalism. In writers like Locke, and later Montesquieu, limited government became the key idea, that is, government limited to securing individual freedom which was viewed as the highest human possibility. In part, this was an expansion of one aspect of the old view of constitutionalism—an emphasis on the rule of law. In its simplest sense, all constitutionalism involves the very idea of law itself, as in the familiar maxim: A government of laws and not of men. Of course, this maxim cannot be understood literally since in fact laws cannot govern of themselves, but always require men to make and execute them, and adjudicate issues arising under them. What is intended is the rule of men *bound* by law, that is, an actual government of men like an ideal government of laws—regular, rational, and aimed at the public interest, rather than arbitrary and based merely upon desire and power. The rule of law entails many things: The network of law constrains all government action, those who govern are also subject to the laws they make, government acts according to known and established procedures and through general laws and policies rather than by specific acts of favoritism or harshness directed against specific individuals. A vital supposition underlies the principle of rule of law: If government follows these procedures, it will tend to do what is intrinsically fair and just. It is believed that procedural regularity somehow tends to yield substantive justice.

But American constitutionalism goes beyond the general idea of a government of laws. It includes specific modern concepts of limited government and, accordingly, specific kinds and techniques of limitation. It holds that these are essentially embodied in the written Constitution, which is the fundamental law that limits ordinary government. This primacy of the Constitution reflects the two major principles of the Declaration of Independence. First, the Constitution is regarded as fundamental law because it embodies the basic will of the people, expressed in their constitutive capacity. That is, the Constitution is *instituted* by *the consent of the governed.* Second, Americans believe that the Constitution provides the major and adequate arrangements necessary to liberty; that is, the Constitution adequately secures the *inalienable rights* of the people. From the force of these two principles the Constitution acquires an immense force in American political opinion, so immense that American government and politics have a peculiarly constitutionalized character.

Limiting the Scope of Government: "The Pursuit of Happiness"

What the Declaration of Independence means by "the pursuit af happiness" indicates an important (and controversial) aspect of the American concept of constitutionally limited government. At a minimum, the Declaration means that men themselves largely have the right to determine wherein their happiness lies rather than have government and the public authorities determine it for them. This involved the great change from traditional political thought that we have already indicated. Until the seventeenth century, most political philosophies rested upon conceptions of natural or divine justice. In these philosophies government's function was to secure justice (not rights) and to assist mankind to achieve the closest possible approximation to what nature or the divine will intended. From this it tended to follow that, in principle, government properly could control every aspect of human behavior. Political authority and not private judgment was made the arbiter of how happiness should be pursued. Above all, this meant a close connection between the political and religious spheres. For example, in the Middle Ages, governmental and quasi-governmental institutions tended to regulate minutely the moral and economic life of the people.

In the sixteenth and seventeenth centuries, these practices had culminated either in corruption or in extreme religious tyranny and savage religious wars. In revulsion, philosophers like Hobbes, Locke, and Montesquieu shifted the emphasis of government from the achievement of justice (which opened the door to the excesses) to the securing of rights.

Where Aristotle had joined state and society into the single concept of the healthy regime, Locke, for example, radically separated the two spheres. The scope of the state or government was thus drastically limited. In Locke's view, the only legitimate functions of the state were those necessary to make possible a peaceful society in which an individual could securely employ his "life, liberty, and estate" as he freely chose.

These new views were reflected in the Declaration's emphasis on rights and thus on the private pursuit of happiness. In the religious sphere, this means tolerance of differences and separation of church and state. In the economic sphere, this means the continuous process of an essentially free play of economic forces. Unquestionably, the American constitutional system presupposes a free, private, commercial society. But this does not mean laissez-faire capitalism. There has never been a time when American economic theory and practice required the absence of governmental regulation. On the contrary, as Madison pointed out, "the regulation of these various and interfering interests," upon which the American system is based, "forms the principal task of modern legislation . . ."[36] But it is, of course, immensely difficult to draw the line between what may and what may not be regulated. Each generation works out its own balance in these matters. But this much must be emphasized: While the Constitution is compatible with a broad range of economic and social practice, it embodies that principle of limited government which rests upon a bias in favor of the primarily *private* pursuit of happiness. Some fundamental limitations on the scope of government are indispensable to the American constitutional system.

Limiting the Powers of Government:
Federalism and the Specific Protections of Liberty

In addition to limiting the scope of government, the American constitutional system involves two other major modes of limitation: the federal division of power between the central and state governments, and the many specific prohibitions and procedural requirements in the original Constitution and the Bill of Rights. These are efforts, not primarily to reduce further the scope or reach of government, but to limit or constrain the powers by means of which government performs the tasks assigned to it. These are of such importance, and have generated so many constitutional and legal aspects of the American political order, that they are reserved for separate consideration in Chapter 4, which is focussed on the powers of the national government.

THE CONSTITUTION: FIXED OR FLEXIBLE?

A written constitution designed to limit the powers of government is subject to two opposite dangers. It may be interpreted so narrowly that it is converted, say, into a fixed and rigid eighteenth-century legal code, doomed to disregard because government cannot then deal with changing political problems. Or it may be interpreted so flexibly that it becomes a mere facade behind which politics operates as it pleases. The two extremes to be avoided are easily stated. But it is difficult in practice to adhere to the mean between the extremes.

Adapting the Constitution

We may find a guide in John Marshall, an early and great Chief Justice of the Supreme Court:

> [This is] a constitution intended to endure for ages to come, and consequently, to be adapted to the various crises of human affairs. To have prescribed the means by which government should, in all future time, execute its powers, would have been to change entirely, the character of the instrument, and give it the properties of a legal code. It would have been an unwise attempt to provide, by immutable rules, for exigencies which . . . can be best provided for as they occur.[37]

In his view the Constitution consists of fundamental principles and arrangements which give the American polity its essential character. These principles and arrangements are so designed as to be capable of guiding conduct in varying circumstances. In any given decade, new practices and new judicial interpretations must be inferred and developed from the constitutional principles for dealing with the problems of that decade. But the Constitution remains the source of fundamentals from which these practices and interpretations are derived. Thus it is adaptable but firm in its essential character. In this lies the strength of the constitutional system. Yet at the same time there is the unavoidable risk that under guise of adaptation to changing circumstances the Constitution may in effect be distorted and ultimately scrapped. The task is always to judge whether a proposed innovation is consistent with the basic constitutional order. This depends upon whether the innovation conforms to the essential principles of the order. To judge wisely requires of each generation a renewed understanding of the constitutional design.

Changing the Constitution

The Constitution is "adapted to the various crises of human affairs" by judicial interpretation, by executive and legislative actions that go unchallenged and become constitutional custom, by shifting public opinion and the forces that mold opinion. But it is not enough that the Constitution may be *adapted*; it must also be capable of *change*. The Framers were aware that time might disclose basic inadequacies in the original design which it would be impossible or dangerous to try to interpret away. Accordingly, they provided for amendments to the Constitution.

Some have argued that the amending process was rigged to prevent any real change by enabling a tiny minority to block an amendment. Since three quarters of the states must ratify an amendment, opposition by one quarter of the states plus one kills an amendment. Thus, *bare* majorities in the 13 *least populous* states could block an amendment desired by overwhelming majorities in the 37 most populous states. Conceivably, then, a tiny fraction of the national popular vote would prevail against the democratic majority. This 'scare arithmetic' has been an important argument for those who have regarded the Constitution as undemocratic. But turn the arithmetic around. Bare majorities in the 38 least populous states can *pass* amendments against the opposition of overwhelming majorities in the 12 most populous states. A national minority can pass an amendment. In short, the requirement of an extraordinary numerical majority of states does not mean an extraordinary national popular majority.

The real aim and practical effect of the complicated amending procedure is not to give power to minorities, but to require *nationally distributed* majorities. It is only accidental that the procedure contains the possibility of a minority blocking (or passing) an amendment. The aim of requiring nationally distributed majorities is to insure that no amendment could be passed simply with the support of a few populous states or sections. In this sense, this was another concession to the 'pure federalists' who feared dominance by the great states. And, harking back to multiplicity of interests, it was also hoped that a nationally distributed majority, engaged in the solemn process of constitutional amendment, would favor only necessary and useful amendments. The solemn process also prevents, as was hoped, such a proliferation of amendments as would make the Constitution the patchwork of carelessly conceived amendments which many state constitutions have become. There have been only 25 amendments in nearly two centuries, indeed only 15 if the original Bill of Rights is subtracted. Adaptation rather than change has been the system's main mode of adjustment to changing circumstance.

In short, the amending process is another example of a device, compatible with democracy, that tends to preserve constitutionalism while empowering government to face its problems competently.

To sum up: The underlying aim of the constitutional system is, upon the basis of democracy, to render government adequately powerful and competent to its tasks, and yet to guard effectually against perversion of the power that has to be granted. We have been examining the principal elements of that power and that effectual guard. *Democracy:* "Final social power" rests with majorities. *Multiplicity of interests and sects:* Majorities emerge only by coalition from a special kind of economic and social diversity. *Representation:* Government is conducted by representatives, selected in ways that foster judgment and skill. *Separation of powers and bicameralism:* Government offices are arranged so as to retard, guide, and thereby moderate democratic will. *Constitutionalism and limited government:* The scope of government and the exercise of its political power are constrained by the constitutional system.

BIBLIOGRAPHICAL NOTE

The two most important works on the American political order, as the frequent references to them attest, are *The Federalist* and Tocqueville's *Democracy in America.* Many readings suggested at the end of the previous two chapters are, as their titles indicate, relevant here as well.

The subjects dealt with in this chapter are major themes in political philosophy. Accordingly, any number of the great political philosophers may be recommended here for further reading. Aristotle's *Politics* is perhaps at once the most difficult and the most comprehensive and profound. The writings of Hobbes, Locke, and Montesquieu are among those most relevant to the study of American problems. Introductory essays on them (and on other writers mentioned in this book) may be found in *History of Political Philosophy,* Leo Strauss and Joseph Cropsey, eds. (2nd ed. 1972)

Regarding problems of democracy generally, a variety of points of view are presented in: Henry Steele Commager, *Majority Rule and Minority Rights* (1944); Robert A. Dahl, *A Preface to Democratic Theory* (1956); Martin Diamond, "Democracy and *The Federalist:* A Reconsideration of the Framers' Intent," in the *American Political Science Review* (March, 1959); R. A. Goldwin and W. A. Schambra, eds., *How Democratic Is the Constitution* (1980); Willmoore Kendall, *John Locke and the Doctrine of Majority Rule* (1941); Herbert McCloskey, "The Fallacy of Absolute Majority Rule," *Journal of Politics* (November, 1949); and Yves Simon, *Philosophy of Democratic Government* (1951). The student will find in these works many suggestions for additional readings.

Two famous studies of representative government are: Edmund Burke, "Speech to the Electors of Bristol" (1774) and John Stuart Mill, *Considerations on Representative Government* (1861). C. H. McIlwain, *Constitutionalism, Ancient and Modern* (1947) is a useful introduction to problems of constitutionalism. M. J. C. Vile, *Constitutionalism and Separation of Powers* (1967) can also be consulted. For an analysis of separation of powers theory consult

Martin Diamond, "The Separation of Powers and the Mixed Regime," and Ann Stuart Diamond, "The Zenith of Separation of Powers Theory: The Federal Convention of 1787," in *Publius* (Summer 1978).

Arthur N. Holcombe, *Our More Perfect Union* (1950) analyzes the American political system in terms of the principles of the Framers. Conyers Read, ed., *The Constitution Reconsidered* (1969) is a collection of essays that deal with many of the subjects of this chapter. A new history of the period is Gordon S. Wood, *The Creation of the American Republic, 1776-1787* (Chapel Hill: University of North Carolina Press, 1969). On the principles of the founding see Robert H. Horwitz, ed., *The Moral Foundations of the American Republic.* For essays on the founders and their intellectual horizons see Douglass G. Adair, *Fame and the Founding Fathers* (1974).

On the relationship between the American Constitution and capitalism, see R. A. Goldwin and W. A. Schambra, eds., *How Capitalistic Is the Constitution* (1981), Walter Berns, "The Corporation's Song," in *The American Spectator* (September 1980), and Irving Kristol, *Two Cheers for Capitalism* (1977).

See Martin Diamond, *The Electoral College and the American Idea of Democracy* (1977) for an account of an evolved institution and the principles of the American system.

NOTES

[1]Tocqueville, *Democracy in America*, I, 270.

[2]June 6 at the Constitutional Convention (emphasis added).

[3]The present move to abolish the 'undemocratic' Electoral College is a practical example. The hostility to the 'Madisonian Model' in contemporary political science is an example of how the study of politics is influenced by the view that the Constitution is undemocratic.

[4]Ironically, this view is shared by many modern conservatives and liberals alike; indeed, the farther to the right or left one goes, the more likely one is to encounter it. Both believe that the original Constitution deliberately hamstrung majority rule, but has been radically democratized by the political process. They differ, of course, in that the one disapproves and the other approves the change. See Martin Diamond, "Conservatives, Liberals, and the Constitution," in R. A. Goldwin, ed., *Left, Right, and Center* (Chicago: Rand McNally and Co., 1965).

[5]This is to apply to the Framers the fine phrase used to describe the aim of Tocqueville's book. See G. W. Pierson, *Tocqueville in America* (New York: Anchor Books, 1959), p. 112.

[6]Tocqueville, I, 262.

[7]See a discussion of this question by Hans J. Morgenthau and Howard B. White in the *American Political Science Review*, LI, No. 3 (September, 1957), 714-33.

[8]See, e.g. Felix Morley, *Freedom and Federalism* (Chicago: Henry Regnery Co., 1959), especially Chapter 1.

[9]See also *Federalist* 39, pp. 240-41.

[10]Alexander Hamilton, *Writings*, H. C. Lodge, ed. (12 vols.; New York: Putnam, 1904), II, 92 (italics omitted).

[11]This quotation is from *Federalist* 51; all unidentified quotations in this section are from *Federalist* 10, the major presentation of the extended-republic theory. Notice that, in its argument, extension is based exclusively on the representative principal and not on federalism.

[12] *The Republic of Plato*, Allen Bloom, trans. (New York: Basic Books, 1968), p. 100.

[13] He used the phrase in the title of his interesting novel, *Sybil, Or the Two Nations* (London: Penguin Books, 1954).

[14] Quoted in Daniel Bell, *The End of Ideology* (New York: Collier Books, 1961), p. 67 (italics in original).

[15] Small countries with dense population and an active foreign commerce can have advanced economies and achieve the useful multiplicity, and large countries can have agricultural, undifferentiated economies. Consider the vast Asian countries until recent years. But in general, largeness is correlated with variety of economic activity.

[16] Although there are profound differences regarding size and kind of economy envisaged, a passage in Aristotle may suggestively be compared with Madison:

> Where the middle class is large, there is least likelihood of faction and dissension among the citizens. Large states are generally more free from faction just because they have a large middle class. In small states, on the other hand, it is easy for the whole population to be divided into only two classes; nothing is left in the middle, and all—or almost all—are either poor or rich.

Aristotle's Politics, Ernest Barker, trans. (New York: Oxford University Press, 1962), Book IV, Chapter 11, p. 182.

[17] *Federalist* 51, p. 324. On the relationship of religious multiplicity to a modern commercial society, it is useful to compare Adam Smith, with whose work Madison was familiar. See especially pp. 744-46 in *The Wealth of Nations* (New York: The Modern Library, 1937).

[18] *Lettres philosophiques,* Raymond Naves, ed. (Paris: Garnier, 1964), p. 29.

[19] *Federalist* 57, p. 350.

[20] The key word here is "inclines." The system tends to produce that result, it does not guarantee it. Obviously, many wretched men are sent to Congress; often from districts with a single dominant interest, but often also from very diversified districts. No constitutional arrangement can guarantee excellent results; politics is not a question of foolproof engineering. Rather, the proper question is always: does the system tend or incline to produce the result it seeks?

[21] Max Farrand, ed., *The Records of the Federal Convention of 1987.* I, p. 50.

[22] But see Paul Eidelberg, *The Philosophy of the American Constitution* (New York: The Free Press, 1968) who expressly disagrees with the argument on which this book is based. Eidelberg argues that in encouraging merit the Constitution provided not a democratic but a traditional *mixed* regime. Eidelberg seems to think that any effort to make democracy decent is incompatible with democracy; in making them mixed regime theorists, Eidelberg makes the Framers 'ancients' rather than 'moderns,' and regards as false Madison's proudest claim that the Constitution remained faithful to the spirit and form of popular government.

[23] *Federalist* 58, pp. 360-361.

[24] Letter to John Taylor, May 28, 1816, *The Works of Thomas Jefferson,* P. L. Ford, ed. (New York: G. P. Putnam's Sons, 1905), XI, 531.

[25] The main contemporary criticisms of the Electoral College have centered on the "winner-take-all" general ticket aspect, which was a nineteenth century extra-constitutional development.

[26] *Federalist* 57, p. 351.

[27] The Constitution makes no provision for separation of powers in the state governments. This was naturally left to the state constitutions. However, the doctrine has been so completely accepted that all the state governments have always maintained some form of separation of powers.

[28] *Federalist* 47, p. 301.

[29] See Aristotle's *Politics,* Book IV, chapters 14-16. Useful studies of the separation of powers are: W. B. Gwyn, *The Meaning of Separation of Powers* ("Tulane Studies in Political Science," The Hague: Martinus Nijhoff, 1965), and M. J. C. Vile, *Constitutionalism and Separation of Powers* (Oxford: Clarendon Press, 1967).

[30] The legislature also inevitably shares in this mixture of powers. For example, the Senate shares in the presidential powers of appointing Federal officers and making treaties; Congress as a whole creates, supports, and to a degree controls the executive departmental organizations.

[31] *Federalist* 51, pp. 321-22.

[32] *Federalist* 63, p. 384.

[33] For an excellent understanding of this solution see Justice Gibson's dissent in *Eakin* v. *Raub,* 12 Sergeant & Rawle (Pa. S. Ct., 1825) at 350, 351.

[34] Farrand, *op. cit.,* III, 133.

[35] *Federalist* 63, p. 383.

[36] *Federalist* 10, p. 79.

[37] *McCulloch* v. *Maryland,* 4 Wheat. U.S. 316 (1819).

Chapter 4

THE CONSTITUTIONAL SYSTEM

It is a melancholy reflection that liberty should be equally exposed to danger whether the Govt. have too much or too little power, and that the line which divides these extremes should be so inaccurately defined by experience.

—MADISON[1]

. . . let a day be solemnly set apart for proclaiming the charter; let it be brought forth placed on the divine law, the word of God; let a crown be placed thereon, by which the world may know, that so far we approve of monarchy, that in America THE LAW IS KING. For as in absolute governments the King is law, so in free countries the law ought to be king; and there ought to be no other. But lest any ill use should afterwards arise, let the crown at the conclusion of the ceremony, be demolished and scattered among the people whose right it is.

—PAINE[2]

The tendency to constitutionalize all political issues is a distinguishing characteristic of the American polity. The official Constitution is so central to American political life that it affects the very way Americans address themselves to political matters. For example, Americans usually ask *two* questions about public policy where citizens of other countries usually ask only *one*: Others simply ask *ought* their national government do this or that; Americans ask also *may* ours do it under the Constitution. It is not enough in American politics, as it is elsewhere, to decide whether it is wise or advantageous to do something; we also consider whether the Constitution permits the thing to be done at all, or by which level of government, and by what procedures the thing may be done constitutionally. This threefold division of our *may* question anticipates three major concerns of this chapter: ours is a constitutional system of delegated and enumerated powers, in a 'federal and national compound,' under specific constitutional protections of liberty.

A peculiar American word usage also points to the constitutionalizing tendency indicated by our double ought-we-may-we question. We usually speak of the powers of government, not, as a European might, of its power. This suggests the extent to which we differ from most other polities in our conception of governing power. They tend to conceive of governing power as a single undifferentiated mass; we conceive of our national government as depending upon particular constitutionally allocated powers. This effort to govern ourselves according to particular grants and limitations of power contributes greatly to the unique importance we give to our Constitution and to the modes of thought and institutions it generates.

By *constitutionalization* we mean that our political controversies tend to assume the form of disputes over the meaning and nature of the fundamental document. This constitutionalization has immense consequences; it is an extraordinarily ubiquitous determinant of American political behavior. And above all, it tends to moderate political controversy. Political forces align themselves as rival interpretations of an agreed upon constitutional regime, rather than one side defending and the other attacking the regime itself. Constitutional interpretations are frequently vulgar and even transparent rationalizations of underlying interests and ideological preconceptions. Nevertheless, the necessity and habit of putting one's views forward as an interpretation of the Constitution sets bounds to those views, and tends to moderate and hold them within the constitutional channels.

In almost every aspect of our government and politics and in almost every episode of our history, disputes over the meaning of the Constitution have been near the center of the political stage. The constitutional issues involved in the Louisiana Purchase, the Civil War, the rise of industrialism, the New Deal and the welfare state, and in racial segregation and discrimination come readily to mind. The powerful grip the Constitution came almost instantly to exercise on the American mind gave rise to the constitutionalization of our politics; and that constitutionalization persistently keeps the Constitution before our eyes. Thomas Paine's wish, quoted at the opening of this chapter, has been more than granted. He proposed only an annual ritual to "proclaim the charter"; the importance of the Constitution is proclaimed in a thousand ways in our daily political life. How apt then is this English comment on American politics:

> At the first sound of a new argument over the United States Constitution and its interpretation, the hearts of Americans leap with a fearful joy. The blood stirs powerfully in their veins and a new lustre brightens their eyes. Like King Harry's men before Harfleur, they stand like greyhounds in the slips, straining upon the start. Last week, the old buglenote rang out, clear and thrilling . . . .[3]

To speak of the "buglenote" of constitutional controversy is, of course, to think immediately of the United States Supreme Court and of constitutional law, which consists of those legal decisions in which sections of the Constitution are elaborated upon by the judiciary. The importance of the judicial branch in American government is, indeed, another consequence of the constitutionalization of American politics. But to think of the Court as the only important participant in constitutional controversy is to miss the whole point. In the sense we are using the term, constitutionalizaion can occur any place in American political life, at any level of government, in any branch of government, and in the life of parties and interest groups as well. Thus so deeply and uniquely does the official Constitution affect the style and substance of American government and politics.[4]

Recognition of this distinguishing characteristic of the American political order enables us to see its consequence. It is this. The constitutional system—including both the document itself and the informal constitutionalization we have been describing—amounts to a salutary constraint upon the exercise of massive governing power. This is our primary concern in this chapter. Notice that we do not present the system simply as a *constraint* upon power; we give equal emphasis to the massive *governing* power. In this we follow Madison as quoted at the opening of this chapter: Liberty is endangered as much by too little power as by too much power. Thus we construe the Constitution as drawing the line that "divides these extremes"; hence the limitations of a constitutional system make possible a powerful national government that is not dangerous to liberty. In this chapter we examine the way the constitutional system as a whole operates to this end; and we examine especially those aspects of the system that bear most directly upon that end—namely, the national powers; the problems of the federal system; and the specific protections of liberty contained in the original Constitution, the Bill of Rights, and the subsequent amendments.

THE DOCUMENT

The original Constitution is characterized by economy of words, overall brevity (it is only 5400 words), general language, and a concern with fundamental problems that makes it seem timeless. These qualities make it accessible to all. Except for a few passages, an ordinary political man may get directly at the document's main features (and hence engage in disputes about them). And the document does not bog down in eighteenth century details; it speaks to perennial political problems. Some of the Constitution's vast influence on American life is due to these qualities. Although it uses some familiar common law expressions, it is the political document par excellence: "an act of extraordinary legislation, by which the people establish the structure and mechanism of their government; and in which they prescribe fundamental rules to regulate the motion of the several parts."[5]

The Preamble

The document begins with one of its few flourishes, a brief and eloquent statement of purpose traditionally called the Preamble. Its opening phrase, "We, the people of the United States," implies that the national government was created by the people directly, and not by the states as preexisting sovereignties. (The latter would have permitted the construction that the Constitution was a merely federal compact among the states; whereas the "we, the people" formulation rested the national government's powers on the strongest possible foundation, the consent of the governed.) Reference is sometimes made to the Preamble's broad statements of the objects of Union in order to support broad views of the national powers.[6] After the Preamble, the Constitution, exclusive of amendments, is divided into seven parts or articles. Each deals with one general subject.

The First Three Articles:
Separate Organs of Government and Basic National Powers

The first three articles deal with Congress, the Presidency, and the judiciary, respectively, and are hence commonly called the legislative, executive, and judicial articles. Here the fundamental powers are granted and the three great branches constituted. The term separation of powers does not appear in the Constitution, but the very form of the document establishes the separation of powers. Each branch has a separate article and is separately empowered, thus creating three departments of equal (or coordinate) rank. The three articles follow the same general pattern: Each confers its branch's powers, indicates the mode of their exercise, and sets some restrictions on them. Each decrees the structure of its branch, lists its principal offices, and provides for the selection of persons to fill them. Aristotle remarks that a constitution is an arrangement of offices; that is, the way "a citizen body distributes office"—the kinds of authority it establishes and those to whom it gives that authority—determines the characteristics of that country's regime or polity.[7] These three articles constitute the basic frame of the national government.

Article I: the legislative power. Article 1 is the longest and most detailed of all, partly because it contains the bulk of the whole government's grants of power, and many of the limitations. Section 8 is an enumeration of most of the grants, and section 9 of the limitations. Section 10 is devoted to various limitations upon the states, largely designed to protect the national powers from state interference. The article also sets forth in detail the mode of election and the organization of Congress.

A glance at the Constitution reveals an essential characteristic of the government thus constituted: legislative supremacy. The legislative branch is the very first to be constituted and is assigned most of the decisive powers of government. In doing this, the Framers were following John Locke, whose very definition of political power implies the supremacy of the legislative function.[8] Had they not thus assumed that to govern is primarily to legislate, the Framers might well have begun their Constitution quite differently. They could first have listed the general powers or objects of the central government, and then have created separate branches to legislate, execute, and adjudicate with respect to these objects. This would have reduced the legislative branch to being but one of three sharers in the general authority of government. Rather, the Constitution lodges the primary powers of government directly in the legislative branch. As *The Federalist* observed: "In republican government, the legislative authority necessarily predominates."[9]

Article II: the executive power. But while the legislative authority necessarily predominates, the executive branch need not be a mere agent of the legislature. As we saw in the discussion of the separation of powers (pp. 85-95), the Framers deliberately laid the basis for a powerful Presidency.

The general executive power is "vested in a President of the United States," whose mode of election and eligibility to office are then described. In addition the article assigns various specific powers to the President. He is given important military and diplomatic functions; but it must be remembered that his authority in foreign affairs is constitutionally shared with the Congress. On the other hand, he is also specifically assigned a share in legislative matters: In addition to the veto power, assigned to him in Article I, he is also empowered to report on "the state of the Union" and recommend to Congress "such measures as he shall judge necessary and expedient." American political life has been characterized ever since by struggles between an independent executive with great power potential and the supreme legislature.

Article III: the judicial power. This article establishes an independent co-ordinate judicial branch of government by vesting the judicial power in "one Supreme Court, and in such inferior courts as the Congress may from time to time ordain and establish." Holding their offices "during good behavior," federal judges have, in effect, life tenure. The article specifies the jurisdictions the federal courts may exercise, and gives Congress regulatory power over these jurisdictions. The grant of the judicial power is not an unlimited grant, but is sufficiently broad to extend to those conflicts that arise as a consequence of federalism, and to matters where a national interest is involved. This article also includes the definition of treason and the requirement of jury trials for all crimes tried in federal courts. The judicial article is the shortest of the first three articles, but upon this base there has emerged the most powerful judiciary ever known.

The Last Four Articles

Article IV: the 'federal' article. "This article, sometimes called 'the Federal Article,' defines in certain important particulars the relations of the states to one another and of the National Government to the States."[10]

Article V: amendment of the Constitution. The method by which the Constitution can be amended can only be exercised by a blend of Congressional and state action. Thus both the states and the nation participate in changing the fundamental document. Only one provision cannot now be altered in this way: No state may be deprived of equal suffrage in the Senate without its consent. (The small-republic pure federalists adamantly insisted on this guarantee at the Convention.)

Article VI: the question of supremacy. Article VI contains the famous supremacy clause, whereby the Constitution and the laws of the United States made pursuant to it are declared to be "the supreme law of the land." The clause thus provides the constitutional answer to questions about the federal bond; and all state judges are required to uphold the Constitution and the Laws of the United States, anything in their own state constitutions or laws "to the contrary notwithstanding."

Article VII deals briefly with the means by which the Constitution was to be ratified (see pp.43-45), and need not be considered here.

The Amendments

We do not examine the amendments seriatim in this brief overview of the Constitution as a document, as none is a central structural member of the framework of the government, The Eleventh and Twelfth were early corrections of apparently unintended consequences of the document. The first ten, or the Bill of Rights, and the later Fourteenth Amendment are important restraints on national and state power, and are discussed at the end of the chapter....

THE POWERS OF THE NATIONAL GOVERNMENT: PATTERNS AND CHARACTERISTICS

Two doctrines limit the exercise of the national government's powers. Although they appear in the American Constitution together, they are logically separable for greater clarity. These are the doctrines of *delegated* and of *enumerated* powers. In the American polity, the doctrine of delegated powers is expressed formally in the Tenth Amendment, and the doctrine of enumerated powers is implied at the same time.

> The powers not delegated to the United States by the Constitution, nor prohibited by it to the States, are reserved to the States respectively, or to the people.

The theory of *delegated* powers means that the Constitution was created by the people themselves who, composing the states, parted with a portion of the powers of government—some to the national government, some to the state governments—and kept the rest to themselves. The *enumeration* of powers follows naturally from that part of the delegation theory which holds that 1) power was divided between the two levels of government, and 2) some residual powers remained in the people. Thus the theory runs that the people once had the whole power of government in themselves; and they granted (i.e., *delegated*) a large portion to the national government, but not the whole—only the *enumerated* powers. The means by which this enumerated delegation was accomplished was the Constitution, as Lord Bryce observed in the 1880s:

> The subjection of all the ordinary authorities and organs of government to a supreme instrument expressing the will of the people, and capable of being altered by them only, has been usually deemed the most remarkable novelty of the American system.[11]

The Constitution thus derives its status as "supreme instrument" from the idea of popular sovereignty; or, to use the language of the Declaration of Independence, because the Constitution derived its "just powers from the consent of the governed." By enumeration in their document, the people delegated to the national government not an undifferentiated mass of powers, but only those powers they deemed the proper ones for it to have.

The balance of this chapter deals with two results of the doctrines delegated and enumerated powers: the constitutional, and informal, limitations represented by federalism (dividing the powers of government between nation and states); and the limitations the Constitution and the Bill of Rights place on the exercise of the granted powers. Some of the Bill of Rights concerns those powers reserved to the people; the rest of it establishes further constraints on the exercise of national power. We turn first to the pattern of the legislative (lawmaking) powers vested in the Congress, and then to a consideration of federalism; lastly to the constitutional constraints with special reference to the Bill of Rights.

The Patterns of the Grants: National Functions

At first glance (e.g., Art. I, sec. 8) the powers granted to Congress seem to be a very diverse collection, almost a jumble, with few links among the individual items and little apparent reason for some of them. For example, what relationship—if any—is there between the obviously vast and vital power to "regulate commerce . . . among the several states" and the seemingly trivial power to "fix the standard of weights and measures"? And why should the national government be concerned with the latter anyway?

Actually there is an underlying order. This is an order based on the calculated division of functions between nation and states. From it there emerges a national government that is sufficiently empowered to cope with the functions assigned to it and, further, that has some flexibility for development and adaptation. Of the national functions two stand out.

A national economy. We have seen how important the fostering of an "extended" and "commercial" republic was for the creation of the diverse society of a "multiplicity of interests." The proper extent of government control over the economy has been and is debated; that the economy should be securely commercial, and adequately national and unfragmented is not. The Constitution therefore gives the national government a set of powers appropriate to the task of fostering—and regulating—the requisite truly national economy, a nationwide area in which commerce can freely operate and diverse economic processes and groupings proliferate.

First, Congress has the whole power to regulate interstate and foreign commerce. This is the cornerstone. To it are added other substantial powers to create and protect the nationwide monetary system that a nationwide economy needs, e.g., the powers to create a national postal system and—not so trivial after all—to "fix the standard of weights and measures." Imagine the difficulties for nationwide business if the pound and inch varied from state to state.

Correlatively, the states are placed under limitaions to prevent them from interfering with this national commercial economy. They may not burden interstate commerce with state duties. They may not coin money, "emit bills of credit" (that is, issue paper money), or make anything but gold and silver legal tender; the national monetary system is to be safe from them. And, further, the states may not cripple that legal enforceability of contractual obligations which is essential to a commercial economy; they may not "pass any law impairing the obligations of contracts."

The American economy has of course vastly changed since 1787. But the vital point is this: Although no one could have anticipated the precise developments in industry and technology, the Constitution envisaged and presupposed an essentially modern commercial economy. This helps explain the basic continuity—which this book emphasizes—of the constitutional system. The vast economic developments have not required that the political constitution be superseded. Rather, the developments were able to take place within the constitutional 'frame of government,' by adaptation, and mediated by the system's own creative traditions.

External affairs. The states were never understood, even prior to the Constitution, to have sovereign power over relations with other countries and security against foreign dangers. Accordingly, the chief problem was to make effective the powers which had already been formally assigned to the central government under the Articles of Confederation.

The peculiar American separation and partial mixture of powers (see pp. 85-95) is especially evident in the subtle division of the grants of power over external affairs. Congress is given the principal substantive powers, e.g., to provide and regulate an army and navy; to tax and borrow "to provide for the common defense"; to declare war. But the President's executive power inevitably involves him closely with Congress. Moreover, he also has specific powers that parallel those of Congress. Congress makes the fundamental decisions about the armed forces (whether to have a draft or volunteer army, how large a military program to fund, etc.); but the President is commander-in-chief of the armed forces. Congress has the power to decide with whom to make war; but the President, by his authority to send and receive ambassadors, conducts the diplomacy that leads to or averts wars. And the President has the power to make treaties, but only "by and with the advice and consent of the

Senate." In short, from the outset, the Framers sought to balance
the advantages of executive initiative and leadership with those of
democratic responsiveness and control through Congress.

Modern war and diplomacy have become a gigantic enterprise,
pervading the country's life and consuming a tenth of the national
product, and presidential initiative has grown to dangerous proportions. But foreign affairs are still conducted within the original
constitutional grants of power and by means of the same constitutional arrangement of offices. The conduct of foreign affairs is still
subject to the same clashes of President and Congress, deriving from
the original constitutional design, as it was in Washington's,
Adams', or Madison's presidencies.

The Characteristics of the Grants:
Fullness of Power

The national powers all have some important common characteristics. The theme which organizes these characteristics is that though
the powers have boundaries, within these boundaries they are full
and sweeping; the grants are not made with a timid or a grudging
hand.

First, the national government is *master of its own affairs;* this was,
of course, the principle for which the Framers had contended, when
they rejected a merely federal system (see p. 24 ff). Thus, the
national government does not have to act through the agency of the
states. It can appoint, pay, and control its own officials, and enforce
its laws in its own courts directly on individual citizens. And—an
obvious but important point—it rules its own seat of government.

Second, reflecting the tightly-knit logical structure of the constitutional document, the powers *reinforce* and *complement* each other.
Thus, the national government does not have just the power to
regulate commerce in a general way; it also has powers to regulate
the money in which commerce is conducted, the mail on which it
depends, the bankruptcies which may disturb, and the patents and
copyrights which may stimulate or clog it, and so on.

Third, the major granted powers are supported by some auxiliaries (e.g., the power to coin money is supported by the power to punish counterfeiting); one of the most famous and central of the auxiliaries is the "necessary and proper" clause. The sweep of the language is notable; it empowers Congress to make

> *all* laws which shall be necessary and proper for carrying into execution the foregoing powers, and all other powers vested by this Constitution in the government of the United States, or in any department or officer thereof.[12]

This power's significance, and the significance of the consequent idea of *implied powers,* is revealed in a contrast with the Articles of Confederation. The second of the Articles limited the Confederation to the exercise of its "expressly" delegated powers: That is, what was not said in so many words, the Confederation could not do; it could not derive any powers from the express grants by construction. The Constitution pointedly avoids limiting the national government in this way. Indeed, when the first Congress was considering the Tenth Amendment, some states' rights advocates tried to get the word "expressly" put in; this was rejected by Congress. The national government is therefore not limited to the exact letter of its express powers; it has as well those implied powers which a reasonable construction of the constitutional grants allows.

In short, the characteristics of the national powers display a thrust toward plenary powers, toward authority fully commensurate with the responsibility.

THE NATIONAL GOVERNMENT AND THE STATES

So far we have discussed the national government's powers with almost no reference to the states. With the states off the stage, we have seen a powerful national government. But this government lives constantly in the presence of active and powerful state governments. The two tower up as the overwhelmingly dominant structures in the country's political landscape, and together they largely cause that immense complexity which startles and at first bewilders the student of American institutions....There are two governments, covering the same ground, commanding with equally direct authority, the obedience of the same citizen.[13]

No single fact of American political life is more complex or more productive of the peculiar qualities of American constitutionalism and American politics than the fact of these two governments "covering the same ground." In short—the problems of federalism.

The Conventional Modern Understanding of Federalism

We cannot deal with the problems of federalism until we know precisely what federalism is. That would seem to pose no difficulty since most modern writers agree on its definition.

> By the federal principle I mean the method of dividing powers so that the general and regional governments are each within a sphere, coordinate and independent.[14]

According to this widely shared definition, the essential federal characteristic is simply the division of governing power between member states and a central government, each having the final say regarding matters assigned to its sphere. We have already seen (pp. 24-25) the corollary of this modern definition: Federal government is treated as the mean between the extremes of confederation and national (or unitary) government. Thus, federal government combines states which *confederally* retain sovereignty over certain government tasks, with a central government that is *nationally* sovereign over other tasks.

Federalism must not be confused, as it often is, with the separation of powers. Modern federalism is a system of divided sovereignty; the whole unseparated governing authority respecting certain matters is given to the national government, and the whole unseparated governing authority respecting others to the states. The *separation of powers* refers to the internal organization of a single government; the legislative, executive, and judicial aspects of governing are distributed to separate branches. For federalism, it makes no differ-ence how the national or state governments are internally struc-tured; for the separation of powers, it makes no difference whether the national government has the entire sovereignty, or divides it with the states. Federalism requires the cooperation of two distinct governments in governing the country; the separation of powers requires the cooperation of the branches of a single government in governing the country.

With this distinction in mind, we can see that the American system is the very model of a modern federal system because it constitution-ally divides governing power between the member states and the national government. Indeed, the conventional modern definition of federalism is little more than a slightly generalized description of the American system. But this ignores Madison's well considered warning: "The compound government of the U.S. is without a model, & to be explained by itself, not by similitudes or analogies."[15] We must ponder the ironic fact that the framers of the American political system defined federalism very differently from modern writers; consequently, they did not view the system they designed as merely federal. Rather, they thought that the Constitution was "in strictness, neither a national nor a federal Constitution, but a composition of both."[16] To grasp their understanding of federalism, and of the "compound" they created, we must examine briefly the history of federalism up to the creation of the American system.

The Earlier Understanding of Federalism

Dr. Samuel Johnson's famous eighteenth century dictionary supplies a good clue to the earlier understanding of federalism:

Federal . . . from foedus (faith) . . . Relating to a league or contract.

Confederacy . . . A league; a contract by which several persons engage to support each other; federal compact.[17]

Notice that the terms federal and confederal are treated as perfectly synonymous. And notice, above all, that Johnson completely omits the key element in the modern definition of federalism, namely, the division of the governing power, with important duties being assigned to the national government. In the earlier view, no *governing* power at all is assigned to the central federal body; indeed, in this view, federalism is not a governmental system, but only a contractual relationship dependent upon the good faith of the contracting parties. Thus, pre-modern federal systems did not create a central government at all, but only a league or alliance entered into by autonomous governments to further their mutual interests.

What explains this massive difference between pre-modern and modern federalism? As usual, it is the ends men seek to achieve that make intelligible their political institutions and behavior. Thus, pre-modern and modern federalism differ in two vital respects: first, concerning the ends or the 'mutual interests' to be promoted by a federal system, and, second, the ends the member states seek to achieve by retaining all or part of their sovereignty. In short, any given federal system is always the product of two opposing sets of reasons: the reasons for remaining small and independent, and the reasons for forming some sort of larger union. The differences among federal systems result from the different reasons for wanting federalism. In all pre-1787 federal systems, the reasons for remaining small and independent were powerful, while the reasons for union were less compelling. The two most famous pre-modern approaches to federalism make this clear.

Polis-federalism. The first is the ancient reasoning in favor of federalism. It may be termed *polis*-federalism. This approach to federalism rested upon the Greek view that the worthwhile life could be lived only in very small political communities. Their term for these communities—*polis*—is usually translated as city-state; but the translation blurs the essential point. These were not cities in our modern sense, that is, subdivisions of a larger political whole; rather, they were autonomous (meaning literally self-lawgiving) small countries. The Greeks believed that only in an autonomous polis—no larger, say, than Athens—could men know each other, truly govern themselves, and create the conditions in which the highest human potential could be actualized. Thus the Greeks had a profoundly important reason to preserve the autonomy of each small country: it was *the* pre-condition of the good life. It followed then that any effort to enlarge the political community—to create government on a larger scale—necessarily made life less worthwhile. Thus they could not agree with the modern federal idea that the governing power of the polis should be shared with a larger federal government. They saw federalism primarily as an aspect of foreign policy (an exercise of what John Locke called the "federative power"), namely, a way of dealing with the limited problem of defense and peace.

When we thus examine federalism from the Greeks' own point of view, a different judgment of their notorious 'failure' to develop a strong federal system becomes possible. Most modern writers have reproached the ancient Greeks for lacking the political imagination and practicality to transcend their petty differences and achieve "a more perfect union." But they did not *fail* to form a strong modern federal system; they deliberately *chose not to*, from a philosophic conviction regarding the nature of the good life and the best means to achieve it.

Small republic federalism . . . A bare recapitulation of [small republic federalism] suffices here. In Montesquieu's formulation, republics had to have a small territory for two reasons. First, the virtuous qualities necessary to republican citizenship could only be cultivated in a small republic where "the interest of the public is more obvious, better understood, and more within the reach of every citizen."[18] Second, a large area "supposes despotic authority in the person who governs"; that is, free institutions are incapable of governing great numbers of people in a large area.[19]

Montesquieu's small republic argument resembled the polis-federalism argument but with a decisive difference: Smallness was no longer deemed necessary to the good life in general, but only to republican freedom. Still, this was a profound reason for preserving the autonomy of the small countries forming a federal system, and for drastically limiting the authority of the central federal body.

The associating small republics retained the governing power, and federalism consisted primarily in their voluntary cooperation for limited purposes of mutual defense.

Three principles of pre-modern federalism. Instead of the modern federal principle of dividing power between member states and the national government, the pre-modern theory of federalism developed three operating principles for federal systems. These principles clearly reflect the fundamental reasons upon which premodern federalism was based—namely, reasons for drastically limiting the central authority and preserving the primacy of the member governments:

1. the central federal authority does not govern individual citizens; it deals only with the individual governments that comprise the federal system. Indeed, it does not even govern these; it operates primarily by their voluntary consent to the central decisions.

2. the central federal authority does not deal with the fundamental political problems of the individual governments; all internal matters remain wholly with them. The central federal authority is confined narrowly to certain external tasks of mutual interest to the member states.

3. each individual government has an equal vote in the central federal authority. This equality of suffrage derives from the equality of sovereignty possessed by the individual governments. As it were, no matter what their size or strength or wealth, the individual governments are the equal citizens of the federal system; they are the equal parties to the federal compact.

These are the principles which were embodied in the Articles of Confederation.

The American Federal and National Compound

Since the character of a federal system results from the ends men hope to achieve from it—i.e., their reasons for preserving member state autonomy and their reasons for forming a union—it follows that pre-modern federalism could not be transformed into modern federalism until the reasons for federalism had been transformed. That is precisely what happened in the formation of the American republic.

As we saw in Chapter 3, the great struggle at the Constitutional Convention was between the advocates of a large national republic and those adhering to the small republic theory of federalism. The American small republic theory of 1787 differed from Montesquieu's version; it was a watered down, attenuated small republicanism. Montesquieu had said republics had to be small for two reasons: because smallness generated the citizenly virtues and, negatively, because largeness invited despotism. But in the American small republican theory concern with citizenly virtue tended to drop out; what remained was the concern with inevitable "despotic authority" in the government of large countries. Fear of centralized despotism was the only reason the American small republicans had left for preserving the autonomy of the individual states. It was their only remaining reason for limiting the central authority; on every other count they were prepared to consent to a wholly national government. Clearly this was a far weaker reason than the polis-federalism or authentic small republican reasons for preserving local autonomy. This was a diluted small republic federalism that would accept a very powerful national government, provided its fears of centralized despotism could be assuaged.

That is precisely what Madison and the other leading Framers did at the Convention. They convinced the reluctant delegates that liberty was properly provided for—indeed was more secure—in the large republic established under the Constitution. Moreover, a compromise was reached. The new republic would be both federal and national; more accurately, certain classically federal features were grafted on to the basically national government. The three operating principles of classic federalism were built into some aspects of the new system. For example, the Senate is based upon the traditional federal principle that each member of the federal system has an equal vote in the central authority. The national powers are enumerated, while important power over "internal" matters is reserved to the states. Even the third of these principles —the federal authority deals only with the member states and not individual citizens—has functioned in an important extra-constitutional area, the party system. In the major American political parties, which are organized on quite classically federal lines, the national party authority deals almost exclusively with the state parties as collectivities, rather than with individual party members.

Decentralist federalism. As Tocqueville put it, clarifying Madison's formulation the Constitution established "an incomplete national government, which is neither exactly national nor exactly federal."[20] The American federal-and-national compound became the prototype of modern federalism. Modern federalism, then, is nothing more than an "incomplete national government"—incomplete because all legal power is not lodged in the national government, but is divided between it and the state governments. That is, modern federalism is vestigial classic federalism; the main classic element preserved in modern federalism is that some substantial portion of governing power is constitutionally reserved to the states. The great reason for this division of power which preserves the importance of the states is to guard against the dangers of centralization. In short, modern federalism is a form of decentralization, a way of achieving its advantages.[21]

Indeed the terms decentralization and federalism are now often used interchangeably. But this is a mistake. Federalism is only one way, albeit an excellent way, of achieving decentralization. Wholly national systems, like that of England, may also achieve a salutary degree of decentralization. This simply requires that, although the central government possesses the whole of the legal governing power, it voluntarily devolves to local governmental units the performance of many tasks. This is what Tocqueville called "the system of provincial liberty,"[22] and is the standard situation in most American state governments. But modern federalism requires something more than voluntary decentralization; it requires that the existence and authority of the state governments rest upon a constitutional basis, and that the state governments be, not subordinate, but "coordinate and independent" within their assigned sphere.

The vital point is this: The aim and rationale of modern federalism, as manifested in the American system, is the same as that of decentralization. Decentralization, by devolving functions to local governments, helps to limit the size of the central administrative structure and hence to make it less formidable to liberty. At the same time, decentralization draws masses of citizens into political life by multiplying and simplifying the governments accessible to them, thus activating the citizenry and habituating them to self-government. Further, these local governments become organized structures capable, in case of necessity, of resisting centralized authority or mitigating its excesses. Finally, decentralization permits government to be adapted to local needs and circumstances, and makes possible experimentation in the way problems are met. Decentralization is thus both a vital safeguard to liberty and a way to educate an energetic and competent citizenry.

The American system does not leave something so vital as decentralization to the prudence and volition of the government. Like so much else in the American system, decentralization has been *constitutionalized*. The devolution of functions to the states is not decided upon from time to time as circumstances dictate; rather, the governing power is constitutionally divided. The constitutionally enumerated delegation of powers to the national government, with its consequent reservation of powers to the states, permanently commits the American system in the direction of decentralization. This constitutional division of the governing power generates the peculiar complexities of the American system; it results in a complex system of collaboration and conflict between the national goverment and the states. But the American federal and national compound, for all its inevitable inconsistencies and difficulties, may well be indispensable to achieving the advantages of decentralization in an age when the tendencies to centralization are so powerful.

It is sobering to recall that decentralist federalism—a major American contribution to the art of government—was in a significant sense unintended; the federal elements in the system were forced upon the leading Framers. The American compound resulted from the compromise between the leading Framers, who wanted an essentially unitary national republic, and the adamant small-republic pure federalists. But this confusing compromise of the federal and national principles has generated much that is valuable and unique in American political life during nearly two centuries of development and adaptation.

Conflict and Resolution in the "Federal and National Compound"

The presence of two powerful governments "covering the same ground" is the inevitable consequence of the compromise upon which the system is based. The compound system tries to fit together the national and federal principles, and a distinctive characteristic of the compound is a constant jostling between the two with an equally constant necessity for collaboration and also for resolution of conflicts.

The source of conflict is the clash between the national and federal principles: Both the national government, on the national principle, and the state government, on the federal principle, can and do claim final legal authority over the same citizens. But, since there cannot be two final legal authorities on the same subjects, the American system rests upon a constitutional *division of subjects* over which the two governments have the final say.

Dividing authority between governments encounters great practical difficulties, however. That there are two spheres of authority may well be unchallenged. But three problems arise. First, the two authorities inevitably tend, despite any agreed-upon division, to have overlapping concerns. Second, even reasonable men can and do disagree over what belongs to the nation and what to the states. Third, when there is a collision between the two governments, a method is needed for final resolution of these overlaps, disagreements, and collisions.

The problem of overlapping concerns. Whatever the constitutional division of authority, in performing their respective functions both the national and state governments tend in practice to expand beyond any strict boundaries. It is a natural fact of our style of life and governing that the national and state governments often have concerns that overlap and therefore sometimes clash. The function of public education is one good example. This is unquestionably a matter of state authority in the American system, in contrast to most western European systems where the unitary national government directly operates the public schools. Under state supervision, there are roughly 37,000 school districts in the United States; literally hundreds of thousands of citizens are drawn into the governance of education. State and local control over public education is thus one of our main decentralized institutions. Nonetheless, many of the proper concerns of the national government inevitably draw it into the area of public education.

The ominous troubles that arise over discrimination against Negroes is one painfully real instance. The state is concerned to run its schools in ways it thinks best, and this has often meant segregation and discrimination. But there is a national power (and obligation) under the Fourteenth Amendment to see that all citizens receive "the equal protection of the laws." The federal government's concern with equal protection overlaps with the state's responsibility for public education. Both governments are under intense pressure to act in this hotly controverted area, and both governments are thus drawn into overlapping—and often conflicting—regulation. Such overlapping occurs as well in many less dramatic but still conflicting areas. The national government variously supplies funds, materials, advice, and regulation to school lunch programs, school construction and equipment, teacher training, vocational education, etc. The great state universities developed from nineteenth century federal land-grant legislation. Graduate fellowships are now made available on a large scale under various national defense provisions; and the huge grants of federal defense-related research funds to universities are now the subject of much controversy.

The problem of boundaries: "the question. . . . perpetually arising."
Even when each government tries faithfully to stay within its sphere
and no serious overlap of concerns occurs, there remains the sheer
difficulty of deciding what matters have been assigned to the respective spheres. For example, the Constitution entrusts the power over
interstate commerce to the Congress, but the question remaining in
practice is exactly where does purely *intra*state commerce leave off
and *inter*state commerce begin? Where is the line to be drawn?

The problem was given a classic formulation by Chief Justice
Marshall in the famous case of *McCulloch* v. *Maryland.* No one
disagrees, he said, that there are two spheres and that the national
government is limited to its granted powers. "But the question
respecting the *extent of the powers actually granted,* is perpetually
arising, and will probably continue to arise, as long as our system
shall exist."[23] The classic response to the question dates from the
earliest years of the Republic and is still current: *strict* versus *loose*
construction of the constitutional grants. Strict construction reads
the grants quite literally and attempts to adhere to the letter of the
express words of the document. Loose construction reads the grants
in broader terms of ends desired, which allows a great latitude of
implied powers. Thus, strict constructionists read the "necessary
and proper" clause as granting no more than the power to enact
those laws without which the express powers literally could not be
exercised. Loose constructionists, on the other hand, read the clause
as a broad grant of power in itself, which authorizes any and all
means, not otherwise prohibited by the Constitution, that can effec-
tuate the national powers. These are the extremes of these two
views, which are roughly those of Thomas Jefferson and Alexander
Hamilton, respectively.

In practice, the conflict over interpretations of the scope of national
power has been between the positions of James Madison and John
Marshall, both less extreme than those just described. Madison's
rule for constitutional construction is that if the power was granted
all reasonable implied powers incidental to it might be exercised,
whether or not they interfered with the powers of the states; but if a

substantive power was not granted, it might not be implied via the necessary and proper clause from the existence of any of the granted powers. The Constitution, Madison wrote, should "be expounded indeed not with the strictness applied to an ordinary statute by a Court of Law; nor on the other hand with a latitude that under the name of *means* for carrying into execution a limited government, would transform it into a Government without limits."[24] Madison's principle, in his own language, places him by choice, midway between Jefferson ("the strictness applied to an ordinary statute") and Hamilton ("a latitude that under the name of means . . ."). Marshall's theory, expressed in *McCulloch* v. *Maryland,* is loose construction, but does not go as far as Hamilton's, for it requires a reasonable relationship between constitutional ends and the means employed. It deserves to be quoted both for the theory it states, and because it is generally acknowledged to be the greatest decision in American constitutional law:

> Let the end be legitimate, let it be within the scope of the constitution, and all means which are appropriate, which are plainly adapted to that end, which are not prohibited, but consistent with the letter and spirit of the constitution, are constitutional.[25]

The controversy over the establishment of a National Bank, in 1790-1791, was the first real constitutional debate of the new American nation. It was also the setting in which all four of the theories of constitutional construction we have been considering first appeared. (Marshall's decision in *McCulloch* v. *Maryland,* 1819, upheld the constitutionality of the Bank, from the point of view of the Supreme Court. The Congress had already judged it to be constitutional, as had the President [Washington] at the time of its original incorporation.) What is most remarkable about the controversy is simply taken for granted. But the fact that the Bank controversy took the form of a *constitutional* conflict cannot be assumed as a natural development. In other countries it would have been fought out exclusively—and probably more bitterly—in terms of the economic and political issues that generated the initial disagreements. (It was a question of how best to foster a commercial society, perhaps in part a question of agrarian versus commercial interests, and in part a matter of emerging political alignments later to blossom into the Federalist and Democratic-Republican parties.) The most significant fact about the controversy, therefore, was the deliberate constitutionalization of the issue by the protagonists—Washington, Randolph, Jefferson, Madison, Hamilton, and twenty-seven years later, Marshall. Americans now expect, as a matter of course, that all such disagreements will take the form of debates over constitutionality. We began the chapter by pointing to this central fact of American political life. Yet it was neither necessary nor usual for this to develop; nor was it simply part of an organic growth of constitutionalism in America. This crucial development was largely the product of a conscious determination on the part of the founding fathers to live within the Constitution they had brought into being, and thus to create that necessary veneration and primary importance of the document which now 'constitutes' the limiting framework for the safe exercise of great national powers. In no other dispute is this purpose so clearly apparent as it is in the National Bank controversy.

Similar disputes over the extent of the national powers are a perennial part of American politics. Some who oppose foreign economic aid believe that the national government has no constitutional power to spend money for at least some of this program's purposes.[26] Supporters of the program contend that the power is clearly implied in the expressly granted powers over defense and foreign relations and also, as they read the constitutional language, in the power "to...collect taxes...to pay the debts and provide for the common defense and general welfare of the United States." In truth, the strict construction and loose construction arguments are almost always available, and useful, partisan political weapons. In many concrete situations there is some uncertainty and room for argument about constitutional meanings. However, liberal construction has been the dominant view; indeed, the country has never actually been governed under the strict constructionist view.[27]

The problem of resolving conflict. A method was provided from the outset for the resolution of conflicts between state and nation:

> The General Convention regarded a provision within the Constitution for deciding in a peaceable and regular mode all cases arising in the course of its operation, as essential to an adequate System of Govt.... it intended the Authority vested in the Judicial Department as a final resort in relation to the States, for cases resulting to it in the exercise of its functions (concurrence of the Senate chosen by the State Legislatures, in appointing the Judges, and the oaths & official tenures of these, with the surveillance of public Opinion, being relied on as guarantying their impartiality):...this intention is expressed by the articles declaring that the federal Constitution & laws shall be the supreme law of the land, and that the Judicial Power of the U.S. shall extend to all cases arising under them...[28]

The Supreme Court is thus the final "arbiter of the federal system."

This does not mean that all such conflicts find their way into the Supreme Court nor that every state/nation conflict must be resolved in this manner. What it does mean is that where difficulties are not dealt with in the Congress or elsewhere in the political system, there is a constitutionally provided solution—a "court of last resort." Secondly, the Court itself has varied the theory it applies of the appropriate national-state relationship. Initially and continuing until after the Civil War, the Court followed the constitutionally sound doctrine of Chief Justice Marshall expressed in the case of *Gibbons* v. *Ogden:*

> ...In exercising the power of regulating their own purely internal affairs ...the states may sometimes enact laws, the validity of which depends on their [not] interfering with, and being contrary to an act of congress passed in pursuance of the Constitution....Should this collision exist, it will be immaterial whether those laws were passed in virtue of a concurrent power 'to regulate commerce with foreign nations and among the several states,' or, in virtue of a power to regulate their domestic trade and police. In one case and in the other, the acts of New York must yield to the law of congress...[29]

This famous case involved the Robert Fulton steamboats. The state of New York granted a steamboat monopoly to Ogden. This barred the port of New York City to Gibbons, a New Jersey steamboat operator, and thus excluded him from the developing New Jersey-New York trade. There was no real quarrel here about the respective spheres of authority. No one denied that, if the national power over interstate commerce had not existed, New York could grant the monopoly and regulate New York harbor under her authority over *intra*state commerce. But on the other hand the New Jersey-New York trade was part of *inter*state commerce over which the national government had authority. The question therefore was: When conflicting exercises of legitimate national and legitimate state power put the two governments on collision courses, which of the two must yield the right of way? The Supreme Court's principle of resolution—and it has been the predominant American answer ever since in such circumstances—was ultimate national supremacy.

A second landmark case in which the Court continued to elaborate its theory of the federal relationship, while at the same time holding to the constitutional purpose of ultimate national supremacy, is *Cooley* v. *Board of Wardens*.[30] Here the Court was called upon to judge the legitimacy of a 1789 act of Congress empowering the states to continue to regulate their pilots in ports until the Congress should make provision otherwise. Pennsylvania had done so and its law was challenged on the grounds that the Congress's power to regulate commerce as such deprived the states of all powers to regulate pilotage. The Court decided that Congress had legitimately provided for local legislation on the matter because it was not one requiring national uniformity or uniform regulation. In the latter circumstances, the Court said, "Whatever subjects of this power are in their nature national, or admit only of one uniform system, or plan of regulation, may justly be said to be of such a nature as to require exclusive legislation by Congress."

The two cases supply these rules for the resolution of conflicts between federal and state power, in particular with regard to commerce: that where there is a collision between a legitimate act of

Congress and a legitimate act of a state the latter must give way; and the Congress may provide for varying state legislation over aspects of interstate commerce which are local and particular in nature until the Congress decides to act upon them. However, matters requiring national uniformity by their nature are the exclusive subjects of Congressional legislation. The Court has recognized that the vast bulk of federal questions is handled satisfactorily by the Congress (see p. 142) and that it is only when all other attempts at resolution have failed that the Court plays its final constitutional role.

The rise and fall of a constitutional doctrine, usually called the doctrine of *dual federalism,* shows the Court departing widely from the traditional national supremacy position on the federal union, and illuminates, by its contrast, the true principles.

American states, subject to whatever limitations their own constitutions impose, have a general authority, commonly called the *police power,*[31] to govern their populations. Dual federalism commenced in a new answer that came to be given after the Civil War to an old question about the nation-state relationship: Does the state police power in and of itself limit the national powers? Originally, following the kind of logic we have seen in *Gibbons* v. *Ogden,* the Supreme Court emphasized national supremacy and held that the police power was not such a limitation. But gradually, the Court began to indicate that it was. A well-known example will illustrate this.

In 1916 the national government, acting under the commerce power, forbade by law the shipment in interstate commerce of goods manufactured in factories employing child labor. The law undoubtedly had—and was intended to have—some repressive effect on the employment of child labor. But employment and working conditions are a local matter, subject to regulation by the police power of the state. Here was a clear collision. The Supreme Court held the national law unconstitutional, ruling that the national government could not so exercise the commerce power because the exercise reached into the domain of the state.[32] This was dual federalism; the powers and spheres of the nation and the states were to be kept entirely separate and distinct, by means of the rigid *exclusion* of the national from regulating any matter that was subject to the state power. In a sense this reversed the supremacy clause; that is, when the national authority collided with the state police power, the former was to yield, although the formal theory was of two equally sovereign governments side by side. To say the least, this was a grave constriction of national ability to regulate nationwide problems (and a happy situation for large interests that would otherwise have been subject to national regulation).

But dual federalism met its downfall in the 1930s. The vast and dangerous problems of the Great Depression clearly exceeded state competence and clearly were appropriate subjects for the full exercise of the national powers. The dual-federalism notion of an automatic mechanical limit on these powers irrespective of the facts of the situation began to seem less and less reasonable and more and more a distortion of the Consitution. The Supreme Court returned to a modern form of its earlier view.[33]

States' rights arguments. The usual arguments for states' rights suggest merely that although the national powers are ultimately supreme they should be somewhat more narrowly interpreted or less energetically exercised than they now are. But at various times in American history, including the present, some voices have argued that much more drastic potentialities of state sovereignty and states' rights exist as against the national government. These have explicitly challenged the very principle of national supremacy.

Thus some pre-Civil War advocates of states' rights claimed that a state had a constitutional right to *nullify* any Federal law affecting it—that is, a right to declare such a law null and void as it affected that state. It has also been argued, and is today argued in a few quarters that, similarly, the state has a right to *interpose* when the national government attempts an exercise of powers that the state believes to be unconstitutional and thus to prevent such an exercise within that state.[34]

The doctrine of *nullification* is based on the view that the states are fully sovereign and the Union a merely federal compact of states, with the national authority ultimately subordinate to them. The American Union is no doubt one of indestructible states. These states possess, and are free to exercise, broad powers of government on their own authority and independently of the national powers. But the still best-established principle of the Union is that the national government is not a mere agent or subordinate of the states. The great statement is that of Chief Justice John Marshall in *McCulloch* v. *Maryland:*

> If any one proposition could command the universal assent of mankind we might expect it to be this—that the government of the Union, though limited in its powers, is supreme within its sphere of action. This would seem to result, necessarily, from its nature. It is the government of all; its powers are delegated by all; it represents all and acts for all. Though any one state may be willing to control its operations, no state is willing to allow others to control them. The nation, on those subjects on which it can act, must necessarily bind its component parts.

Strict construction, dual federalism, and nullification are all attempts to make the purely federal aspects of the constitutional system dominant. But the decision of the Constitutional Convention, the basic tradition, and the present tendency are decisively against those attempts.

Law, politics—and ambiguities. That the principle of national supremacy can have harsh applications is apparent in the desegregation problem. Witness the bitter conflict in 1962 over the admission of a Negro student to the University of Mississippi. On the basis of nearly 25 years of gradual development of precedent in education cases, a federal court found that under the Fourteenth Amendment the student was entitled to admission, and directed the university officials to admit him. The state, exercising its many powers over its university and over the peace of its cities, flatly refused to comply. The student's admission was finally accomplished and the court order carried out, but only through a display by the national government of physical force. Bitter rioting followed during which two lives were lost and many persons were injured.

But such stark confrontations of national and state powers, resolved by rigid judicial (and if necessary executive) enforcement of the principle of ultimate national supremacy, are the dramatic exceptions. At least equally important is an undramatic continuous process of conflict resolution through ordinary law and politics—and above all through Congress. In many important areas, the "Court makes the decisive judgment only when—and to the extent that—Congress has not laid down the resolving rule."[35] The interests of the states find such complete expression through the Congress—since Senators are elected from states and Representatives from districts within states—that Congressional decisions always give thorough consideration to state needs. Thus Congress in practice resolves most of the innumerable tensions and conflicts between the nation and the states.

The processes of resolution—in both their dramatic and their undramatic aspects—struggle with two central difficulties. The first is that nation-state issues can touch the political nerve and can summon up all the forces of the nation's political life, because these issues can involve vital questions of who shall rule what and how. As they always have and no doubt always will, regions, states, social classes, interest groups, factions, parties, politicians, all struggle for survival and advantage—and try to quote the Constitution to their purposes.

The second difficulty is that the Constitution permits, even invites, this use and abuse. There can be differing interpretations of the nation-state balance and differing views of just where boundaries between national and state powers lie, because the constitutional compound does combine the potentially conflicting national and federal principles.[36] There are some real ambiguities in the Constitution, in the strict sense of points having double or dubious meaning or of being open to more than one interpretation. There are still more points where, although the general principle is fairly clear, room exists for flexibility and judgment in the application. These ambiguities and flexibilities lead to clashes, but they also give law and politics their opportunity. If everything were clear and simple there could be no solutions, only victories and defeats.

The potentially conflicting national and federal elements of the system have through law and politics found, and will continue to find, new constitutional and practical resolutions that somehow maintain the essential character of the system as a compound. As a matter of governmental and political practice we can see compelling needs for a large, powerful, and vigorous national government, but we can also see some countervailing needs and forces. Regional economic and political interests, fear of centralization, and the tradition of liberty through local autonomy will continue to sustain the federally decentralized and informally decentralized aspects of the system. There is no doubt that the national government is larger, more active, and a more pervasive influence in American life than it was some years ago. But state and local government has also become steadily larger, more active, and more pervasive.[37] We must now examine the practical governing arrangements which arise from the interplay of these powerful national and state governments.

Federalism in Action

As we have seen, the distribution of powers and responsibilities between nation and states produces conflict—doctrinal disputes, clashes of government authority, intense political struggles by various interests, particularly in Congress, and intricate litigation over its formal and legal aspects. It also produces a vast complex of workaday governing in the innumerable tasks carried on by the various levels and agencies of government in forming public policy and administering public affairs.

Every area in the United States (other than the District of Columbia) is governed by both the national government and a state government. Further, each of these governments is divided into separate departments, agencies, and authorities. State government is elaborated into counties, cities, districts, and other subgovernments. All of these subdivisions may (and most do) have their own purposes, programs, officers, offices, funds, exactions, regulations, requirements, prohibitions, peculiarities, ways of doing or not doing things, and all the other trappings of rule. And each may be acting upon the individual inhabitant directly and more or less independently, in a very welter of governing. How is this busy confusion organized, and how does it work?

Separate or intermixed? The conventional view is that national and state functions are quite separable in principle and typically separated in practice, with each government doing its own jobs:

> . . . like a great factory wherein two sets of machinery are at work, their revolving wheels apparently intermixed, their bands crossing one another, yet each set doing its own work without touching or hampering the other.[38]

In this view, each function is to be performed entirely by only one government—for example, defense by the national government, public education by the state, regulation of the instrumentalities of interstate transportation by the national government, regulation of the manufacture of goods (even for interstate commerce) by the state. Further, this view holds that any national participation in state and local functions is contrary to the spirit of the Constitution and tends toward dangerous concentration of power in the hands of the national government, toward undermining the independence of the states, and toward destruction of the American tradition of local autonomy and self-help.

But some experts take a very different view. They see the various functions not only as "apparently intermixed," but as actually intermixed—and properly so. They believe that the typical situation is an actual sharing of functions and an endless process of collaboration in innumerable ways. Indeed, they sometimes urge that the true image of the federal system is not a layer cake, with national, state, and local government functions in separate and distinct layers, but rather a marble cake, with all of the components interspersed throughout.[39] They offer as an example of their view the health officer of a rural county. He is appointed by the state, but under the health officer of a rural county. He is appointed by the state, but under national standards of qualification. His salary comes in part from both state and federal funds, the county supplies an office and some expense money, and a city pays a further part of his salary because he serves as its plumbing inspector. He acts as a federal officer when, acting under federal law, he impounds impure drugs shipped from a neighboring state, as a state officer when, acting under state law, he inspects locally produced foods, and as a local officer when, acting under local ordinances, he inspects local butcher shops.

But the marble cake image can be misleading. Despite their constant and indispensable collaboration, the three levels of government do in fact have important elements of separateness and autonomy. They are legally and structurally separate entities; they respond ultimately to different constituencies; they can pursue sharply separate policies. This separateness remains an important feature of the system even today when the cooperative sharing and intermingling of functions has increased. The cooperation, no matter how habitual, is essentially voluntary. The national and state governments always retain the capacity—legal and practical—to pull in opposing directions or to function separately. But the separateness was no doubt more pronounced in the nineteenth century. Like Lord Bryce in the 1890s, Tocqueville, in the 1830s, had seen considerable separateness:

> two governments, completely separate and almost independent, the one fulfilling the ordinary duties and responding to the daily and indefinite calls of a community, the other circumscribed within certain limits and only exercising an exceptional authority over the general interests of the country.[40]

However, there was significant sharing and intermingling of functions even in the nineteenth century. For example, the national government granted land for state public schools and colleges and supplied money and engineering help for roads and canals built by the states; national and state agencies cooperated on banking and fiscal matters, and national and state law-enforcement officers sometimes worked together.[41]

The rise of cooperation. During the twentieth century, however, there has been a massive (though not entirely uniform or uninterrupted) increase in such intermingling. National regulation of business and industry began at least in the 1880s and has developed ever since, just as industrialization and nationwide business and a national economy have developed, and it has always involved interactions with state and local regulation.

Beginning even earlier, reaching large proportions by 1900 and gigantic ones today, national and state programs of aid to farmers and agriculture and to other special groups have moved almost in step, though most of the money has usually come from the national government. Vast programs of waterway, rail, and road building, social welfare services, education, housing construction, and the conservation and development of natural resources, to name but a few, have been cooperatively developed. Indeed, the number is so great that a complete inventory of all the activities in which the states and the nation are jointly engaged would be almost impossible to make.[42] It is even difficult to obtain any firm figures on their magnitudes. The best-known figure covers only amounts of money actually granted to state and local governments by the national government to aid programs of these governments in which the national government has some interest. These are termed grants-in-aid. In 1902 regular grants to major programs totalled about 3 million dollars; by fiscal 1967 they had grown to nearly 22 billion. The largest programs were (in descending order of size) public welfare assistance, highway construction, agriculture, aid to education, and public health research and services.

Through the remarkably wide range of the grant-in-aid programs and through innumerable other forms of cooperation, we see nation-state-local relationships in virtually every aspect of governing

America. These federal relationships must be continually borne in mind as part of the workaday process of governing.

THE 'CONSTITUTIONAL LIMITATIONS'

A fundamental characteristic of the American constitutional system—its complex effort to constrain, to channel, control, regulate, limit, and hem in the powers of government—is the theme of this chapter. We have just considered the constraints that result from the federal element within that constitutional system. To complete our survey of the system we must now turn to the detailed constraints the Constitution places upon the powers of government. These are traditionally designated the 'constitutional limitations,' and fall generally within the area of civil rights and civil liberties. Since they are numerous and scattered, it is helpful to identify the basic characteristics, and where these are found.

Some limitations are *substantive;* directed against the substance of government powers and barring government from doing certain things, they are positive rights. For example, the First Amendment forbids any national legislation abridging freedom of speech; similarly, no ex post facto law may be passed. Others are *procedural.* These prescribe the methods and the procedures by which powers are to be exercised. For example, the national government's powers to punish crime are subject to the procedural limitation that trials must be by jury, and private property may not be taken for public use without just compensation. Most of the limitations are contained in the Bill of Rights, which originally applied only to the national government. By means of the due process clause of the Fourteenth Amendment, and a process known as "incorporation," the Supreme Court has made the majority of these limitations apply to the states also.[43] The rest of the limitations are located in the original text of the Constitution.

Our presentation of the limitations is...a brief guide to them here...Those we consider here we divide into three groups: those in the Constitution proper; those added by the Bill of Rights; and those added by the Fourteenth Amendment. This division is not for convenience only; it also reflects the pattern of the limitations. While there is overlap, the group limitations tend to share a distinctive character or thrust.

Limitations in the Constitution Proper

Limitations in the Constitution proper are placed wherever in the instrument they are relevant for the original draftsmen's purposes. Since they are therefore scattered, an impression of their overall characteristics is somewhat hard to get at first. On closer inspection, however, pattern and purpose emerge.

Some apply to the internal workings of the government, and are intended to protect these against some specific danger or abuse: An example is in Article III: the "judicial power" can be exercised only in "cases or controversies." The courts will not give general advisory opinions to Congress or the President. This helps to maintain the desirable degree of judicial detachment from direct policy making.[44]

Many limitations are addressed to preserving the basic political characteristics of the system. The prohibition against grants of titles of nobility is a precaution against the creation of a formal aristocracy, inimical to the republican nature of the regime. The prohibition of bills of attainder and ex post facto laws arose from considerations of political liberty, since these had frequently been used in England against political opponents of a regime. The prohibitions of tax preferences or disadvantages for any state are aimed at preserving the federal independence and equality of the states.

There are (e.g., Art. I, sec. 10) limitations applied to the states. Many of these are obviously correlatives of powers granted the national government and are aimed at preventing various possible kinds of nation-state clashes. Others apply to the states some specific protections of political interests and freedoms applied against national action; for example, the states also may not pass ex post facto laws or bills of attainder, nor may they grant titles of nobility.

Some personal rights and freedoms are protected in the body of the Constitution; jury trial and habeas corpus are examples. It is instructive to reflect that all modern totalitarian regimes tamper with or wipe out just such rights as these. The fundamental methods of tyranny do not change much.

The Bill of Rights

Ten amendments were added shortly after ratification (see p. 52); these are the Bill of Rights. Understanding of them begins with their background in eighteenth century Anglo-American legal and political ideas. One fertile source both of their general principles and of their specifics was the view Americans then held of the "rights of freeborn Englishmen." But this was only the beginning. The First Amendment, as its 'father' James Madison said in Congress, protected rights unprotected in the British Constitution. Thus the American Bill of Rights, inspired by English experience, went far beyond the rights of Englishmen. During the last thirty or forty years, the provisions of the Bill of Rights have almost all been the subject of many judicial decisions, much debate, and voluminous and detailed analysis.

The contents of the Bill are divided between two kinds of protections: *procedural,* such as those concerned with criminal prosecutions and other legal actions; and *positive* or substantive, such as the First Amendment freedoms of speech and religion. Positive protections can be understood as conferring or recognizing areas to be freed from government interference; procedural protections are those kinds of provisions which prescribe the manner in which governmental power shall be exercised, so as not to become arbitrary or tyrannical.

The First Amendment freedoms clearly aim in part at protecting a free and democratic political process. But they also protect from governmental repression freedom of religion and much nonpolitical speech and writing—protections appropriate to a society in which happiness is to be privately, and thus freely, pursued. Detailed restraints on criminal procedure are found in several amendments, e.g., the provisions for grand jury indictment, jury trial, assistance of counsel, etc. Some aspects of these protections have effects far beyond criminal cases, however. Thus the Fourth Amendment's interdiction of "unreasonable searches and seizures" is broadly protective of personal privacy against many other kinds of governmental action as well. The main explicit protection for property—so central, as we have seen, to the whole system—is found in the provision of the Fifth Amendment that "No person shall . . . be deprived of life, liberty, or property, without due process of law; nor shall private property be taken for public use, without just compensation." The Amendment's protection of property is understood to be general and has had an extensive and important history. Apart from its application to property, the due process of law clause has been developed by the courts into a powerful and wide-ranging judicial weapon against almost any kinds of official procedures by the police, by government agencies, by Congress, or by any official authority, which the courts regard as seriously unjust or oppressive. An immense body of constitutional law has grown out of this single clause.

Constitutional Limitations on the States: The Fourteenth Amendment

The Bill of Rights applied only to the national government; a further amendment against state interference with some basic liberties was narrowly defeated in the first Senate. Its protections are therefore not available against the state governments.[45] The Fourteenth Amendment, however, has become, in the hands of the Supreme Court, a very copious source of limitations on the states, similar to those of the Bill of Rights.[46]

The Amendment contains two principal protective clauses: the due process clause and the equal protection clause.[47] Each has its own meaning and effect, although the courts do not always distinguish sharply between them. The due process clause here has at least as broad a meaning as that of the due process clause in the Bill of Rights. Further, the equal protection clause is construed as a sweeping prohibition against many kinds of state action which the courts conclude are arbitrary, or seriously discriminatory, or clearly unreasonable. But the two clauses do much more as well, in that through them many of the same protective principles are applied against the states as are applied against the national government through the Bill of Rights. These include the First Amendment freedoms, protection against the taking of property for public use without just compensation, and many that protect persons from unfair or oppressive official procedures.[48]

Taken together, the various constitutional limitations are a broad armory of protections against oppressive government. Most can be and are formally enforced by the judiciary when necessary; this vastly strengthens the general judicial constraint upon the operations of government. But the influence of the constitutional limitations goes far beyond the courtroom. They are a standard by which government is judged. As such, they profoundly influence public opinion and through it the political process and official conduct. This influence is dramatically illustrated in the civil-rights controversy. The Negro and other civil-rights organizations have a powerful political weapon in the simple force of these constitutional limitations. Their very phrases—"the equal protection of the laws," "the right of the people peaceably to assemble," and the like—are impressive statements of American ideals, and make powerful slogans in political struggles.

How these limitations operate in politics and in constitutional law . . . [is not reprinted here]. It suffices here to emphasize that they are vital to the constitutional system. Like the other principles of that system . . . they are among the principles that inspirit the institutions and processes of government to which we now turn.

BIBLIOGRAPHICAL NOTE

On the idea of constitutionalism and its history, see Charles H. McIlwain, *Constitutionalism: Ancient and Modern* (1947); Herman Finer, *The Theory and Practice of Modern Government* (1962); Francis D. Wormuth, *The Origins of Modern Constitutionalism* (1949); and C. J. Friedrich, *Constitutional Government and Democracy* (1950).

Those aspects of constitutional law relevant to this chapter may be studied further in the following works which deal with constitutional law in general. Alfred H. Kelly and Winfred A. Harbison, *The American Constitution: Its Origins and Development*, 3rd ed. (1963) is a standard history of American constitutional law. C. Herman Pritchett, *The American Constitution*, 3rd ed. (1977) is a valuable general guide. See also Edward S. Corwin, ed., *The Constitution of the United States: Analysis and Interpretation* (1953).

Some of the classical theoretical works on federalism and decentralization, like *The Federalist*, Tocqueville, and Bryce, have been mentioned throughout the chapter; the reader is reminded of their indispensability. See also John C. Calhoun, *Disquisition on Government*. Guidance to many other relevant writings is to be found in Walter H. Bennett, *American Theories of Federalism* (1964).

Modern general works on federalism are K. C. Wheare, *Federal Government*, 3rd ed. (1962); Arthur W. MacMahon, ed., *Federalism: Mature and Emergent* (1955); G. C. S. Benson et al., *Essays in Federalism* (1961); and A. Maass, ed., *Area and Power* (1959). Robert A. Goldwin, ed., *A Nation of States* (1963) is a collection of essays of contrasting viewpoints.

Valuable accounts of American federalism are Morton Grodzins, *The American System*, edited by Daniel J. Elazar (1966); M. J. C. Vile, *The Structure of American Federalism* (1961), and Aaron Wildavsky, *American Federalism in Perspective* (1967). Henry M. Hart, Jr. and Herbert Wechsler, *The Federal Courts and the*

Federal System (1953) is an excellent casebook on federal jurisdiction. For the role of the states, see Daniel J. Elazar, *American Federalism: A View from the States* (1966).

NOTES

[1] James Madison to Thomas Jefferson, Oct. 17, 1788, in *Writings,* V, 272.

[2] Thomas Paine, *Common Sense,* in P.S. Foner, ed., *The Complete Writings of Thomas Paine* (New York: The Citadel Press, 1945), p. 29.

[3] The London *Economist,* May 10, 1952, commenting on President Truman's seizure of the steel mills during the Korean war. The passage is quoted in Alan F. Westin, *The Anatomy of a Constitutional Law Case* (New York: The Macmillan Company, 1958).

[4] We do not find in the Constitution mention of parties, interest groups, lobbyists, Congressional committees and chairmen, state and city political bosses and machines, etc.; but to a decisive extent such governmental and political forces emerge from, are shaped by and rest upon, the official Constitution which grants powers, prescribes how they shall be exercised, and defines the federal relationship between the national government and the states. In short, the formal Constitution is an important determinant of informal, extra-constitutional political behavior.

[5] Justice Gibson of Pennsylvania in *Eakin* v. *Raub,* 12 Sergeant & Rawle (Pa. S. Ct., 1825), at 347.

[6] For a controversial argument that the Preamble had great legal significance see William W. Crosskey, *Politics and the Constitution in the History of the United States* (Chicago: University of Chicago Press, 1953), I, 363-379.

[7] Aristotle's *Politics,* trans. E. Barker (New York: Oxford University Press, 1962), Book IV, chapter 3, section 5, p. 161.

[8] *"Political Power* then I take to be a Right of making laws with Penalties . . . , and of employing the force of the Community, in the Execution of such Laws. . . ." *Two Treatises of Government,* ed. Peter Laslett (New York: Mentor Books, 1965), p. 308.

[9] *Federalist* 51, p. 322.

[10] Edward S. Corwin, *The Constitution and What It Means Today* (New York: Atheneum, 1963), p. 159. See also the much longer version of this excellent work, *The Constitution of the United States of America: Analysis*

and *Interpretation* (Washington, D.C.: Government Printing Office, 1953), which is a prerequisite to any study of the Constitution.

[11] James Bryce, *The American Commonwealth* (2 vols.; 3rd ed.; New York: The Macmillan Company, 1889), I, 37.

[12] Art. I, sec. 8. Emphasis added.

[13] Bryce, *op. cit.*, I, 17-18.

[14] K. C. Wheare, *Federal Government* (3rd ed.; London: Oxford University Press, 1962), p. 11.

[15] James Madison, "Outline," *Writings*, IX, 351 (1829).

[16] *Federalist* 39, p. 246.

[17] *Dictionary of the English Language* (2 vols.; Heidelberg: Joseph Englemann, 1828).

[18] *The Spirit of the Laws*, Book VIII, chapter 16. For a profound understanding of Montesquieu on the relation of virtue and liberty, see Leo Strauss, *What is Political Philosophy?* (Glencoe, Ill.: The Free Press, 1959), pp. 49-50.

[19] *Ibid.*, Book VIII, chapter 19.

[20] *Democracy in America*, I, 159.

[21] See Martin Diamond, "On the Relationship of Federalism and Decentralization," in Daniel J. Elazar et al., ed., *Cooperation and Conflict* (Itasca, Ill.: F. E. Peacock Publishers, 1969), pp. 72-81.

[22] *Democracy in America*, I, 100. See also above, pp. 21-22.

[23] *McCulloch v. Maryland*, 4 Wheat. (U.S.) 316 (1819). Emphasis added.

[24] Letter to M. L. Hurlburt, May 1830, in *Writings*, IX, 371. Emphasis added.

[25] 4 Wheaton 316, 421. Contrast this with Hamilton's view: "Every power vested in a government is in its nature *sovereign*, and includes, by *force* of the *term*, a right to employ all the means requisite and fairly applicable to the attainment of the ends of such power, and which are not precluded by restrictions and exceptions specified in the Constitution, or not immoral, or not contrary to the *essential ends* of political society." *The Works of Alexander Hamilton*, Henry Cabot Lodge, ed. (New York: G. P. Putnam's Sons, 1904), Ill. 446.

[26]E.g., Barry Goldwater, *The Conscience of a Conservative* (New York: Hillman Books, 1960), p. 98.

[27]See, e.g., Harry V. Jaffa, "The Case for a Stronger National Government," in Robert A. Goldwin, ed., *A Nation of States: Essays on the American Federal System* (Chicago: Rand McNally & Company, 1963), p. 119. But see Alfred H. Kelly and Winfred A. Harbison, *The American Constitution: Its Origins and Development* (3rd ed.; New York: W. W. Norton & Company, 1963), pp. 332-35.

[28]James Madison to Thomas Jefferson, June 27, 1783, in Farrand, *op. cit.,* IV, 83-84.

[29]9 Wheaton (U.S.) 1 (1824).

[30]12 Howard 299 (1851), at 319.

[31]The term is only cognately related to policemen. It signifies the general power of internal government and regulation, and is ultimately from the Greek *polis.*

[32]*Hammer* v. *Dagenhart,* 247 U.S. 251 (1918).

[33]See Edward S. Corwin, "The Passing of Dual Federalism," 36 *Va. L. Rev.* 1 (1950). This otherwise excellent article exhibits an error that many make in analyzing American federalism—the premature report of the death of the states.

[34]See, e.g., James Jackson Kilpatrick, *The Sovereign States: Notes of a Citizen of Virginia* (Chicago: Henry Regnery Company, 1957).

[35]Herbert Wechsler, "The Political Safeguards of Federalism," quoted in *Cases and Materials on Constitutional Law,* ed. N. T. Dowling and G. Gunther (7th ed.; Brooklyn: The Foundation Press, 1965), p. 215.

[36]A famous historical example is John Calhoun and Daniel Webster, both able and learned men, and both firmly and sincerely convinced—of direct opposites. See, e.g., Kelly and Harbison, *op. cit.,* ch. 14.

[37]According to a standard text, state and local government expenditures (which are a useful rough measure) have been moving quite steadily upward. In 1957 they stood at about 11 per cent of Gross National Product; in 1948 the figure was about 7.9 per cent, and in 1929 about 7.3 per cent. The rate of increase has been considerably higher than that of domestic program expenditures of the federal government; federal expenditures on such programs (i.e., exclusive of national security and military and foreign aid programs) increased about 50 per cent and state and local ones about 60 per cent in the 1948-1957 period. And, surprisingly in view of the often-

expressed feeling that the federal bureaucracy is overwhelming, state and local expenditures on such programs are consistently over five times as large as the federal. Charles R. Adrian, *State and Local Governments* (New York: McGraw-Hill Book Company, Inc., 1960), ch. 5.

[38]Bryce, *op. cit.,* I, 325.

[39]See Morton Grodzins, "The Federal System," in *Goals for Americans: The Report of the President's Commission on National Goals* (New York: Prentice-Hall, Inc., 1960). For a fuller statement of Professor Grodzins' views, see *The American System: A New View of Government in the United States* (Chicago: Rand McNally, 1966).

[40]Tocqueville, *op. cit.,* I, 61.

[41]See Daniel J. Elazar, *The American Partnership: Intergovernmental Co-operation in the Nineteenth Century United States* (Chicago: The University of Chicago Press, 1962).

[42]A general survey as of 1955 may be found in the 1955 *Report to the President* of the U.S. Commission on Intergovernmental Relations, ch. 3. See also the continuing reports and studies published by the present Advisory Commission on Intergovernmental Relations.

[43]See M. Glenn Abernathy, *Civil Liberties Under the Constitution* (New York: Dodd, Mead and Co., 1968), pp. 40-45 for a clear description and summary of incorporation via the Fourteenth Amendment.

[44]The question arose in 1793. President Washington, through Secretary of State Thomas Jefferson, asked the Supreme Court to answer a number of questions on international law arising out of the war that was beginning in Europe. The justices declined to do so, mentioning the separation of powers and the fact that they were "judges of a court." The correspondence is quoted in Harold J. Berman, *The Nature and Functions of Law* (Brooklyn: The Foundation Press, Inc., 1958), pp. 65-68. This was consistent with the theory of the judicial power that emerged at the Convention, where a proposal that judges give advice was rejected, along with judicial involvement with policy at any point prior to a case or legal controversy.

[45]In *Barron* v. *Baltimore,* 7 Peters (U.S.) 243 (1833), Chief Justice Marshall held, properly, for the Court that the Bill of Rights applied only against the national government and not against the states. This remains the technical legal situation.

[46]In a long series of important cases, the Court has construed the Fourteenth Amendment as "incorporating" many protections of the Bill of Rights, and hence in effect has made them applicable against the states.

[47]The third protective clause, that relating to privileges and immunities has in effect been construed out of existence by the Supreme Court, beginning with the Slaughterhouse Cases, 16 Wall. (U.S.) 36 (1873).

[48]For a discussion of some of the complexities of the Court's method of "selective" incorporation, see Judge Henry J. Friendly, "The Bill of Rights as a Code of Criminal Procedure," 53 *California Law Review* 1965, pp. 929-956.

THE DECLARATION OF INDEPENDENCE

IN CONGRESS, JULY 4, 1776[1]

THE UNANIMOUS DECLARATION OF THE THIRTEEN UNITED STATES OF AMERICA

When in the Course of human events, it becomes necessary for one people to dissolve the political bands which have connected them with another, and to assume among the powers of the earth, the separate and equal station to which the Laws of Nature and of Nature's God entitle them, a decent respect to the opinions of mankind requires that they should declare the causes which impel them to the separation.—We hold these truths to be self-evident, that all men are created equal, that they are endowed by their Creator with certain unalienable Rights, that among these are Life, Liberty and the pursuit of Happiness.—That to secure these rights, Governments are instituted among Men, deriving their just powers from the consent of the governed,—That whenever any Form of Government becomes destructive of these ends, it is the Right of the People to alter or to abolish it, and to institute new Government, laying its foundation on such principles and organizing its powers in such form, as to them shall seem most likely to effect their Safety and Happiness. Prudence, indeed, will dictate that Governments long established should not be changed for light and transient causes; and accordingly all experience hath shown, that mankind are more disposed to suffer, while evils are sufferable, than to right themselves by abolishing the forms to which they are accustomed. But when a long train of abuses and usurpations, pursuing invariably the same Object evinces a design to reduce them under absolute Despotism, it is their right, it is their duty, to throw off such Government, and to provide new Guards for their future security.—Such has been the patient sufferance of these Colonies; and such is now the necessity which constrains them to alter their former Systems of Government. The history of the present King of Great Britain is a history of repeated injuries and usurpations, all having in direct object the establishment of an absolute Tyranny over these States. To prove this, let Facts be submitted to a candid world.—He has refused his Assent to Laws, the most wholesome and necessary for the public good.—He has forbidden his Governors to pass Laws of immediate and pressing importance, unless suspended in their operation till his Assent should be obtained; and when so suspended, he has utterly neglected to attend to them.—He has refused to pass other Laws for the accommodation of large districts of people, unless those people would relinquish the right of Representation in the Legislature, a right inestimable to them and formidable to tyrants only.—He has called together legislative bodies at places unusual, uncomfortable, and distant from the depository of their public Records, for the sole purpose of fatiguing them into compliance with his measures.—He has dissolved Representative Houses repeatedly, for opposing with manly firmness his invasions on the rights of the people.—He has refused for a long time, after such dissolutions, to cause others to be elected; whereby the Legislative powers, incapable of Annihilation, have returned to the People at large for their exercise; the State remaining in the mean time exposed to all the dangers of invasion from without, and convulsions within.—He has endeavoured to prevent the population of these States; for that purpose obstructing the Laws for Naturalization of Foreigners; refusing to pass others to encourage their migration hither, and raising the conditions of new Appropriations of Lands.—He has obstructed the Administration of Justice, by refusing his Assent to Laws for establishing Judiciary powers.—He has made Judges dependent on his Will alone, for the tenure of their offices, and the amount and payment of their salaries.—He has erected a multitude of New Offices, and sent hither swarms of Officers to harrass our people, and eat out their substance.—He has kept among us, in times of peace, Standing Armies, without the

Consent of our legislatures.—He has affected to render the Military independent of and superior to the Civil power.—He has combined with others to subject us to a jurisdiction foreign to our constitution, and unacknowledged by our laws; giving his Assent to their Acts of pretended Legislation:—For quartering large bodies of armed troops among us:—For protecting them, by a mock Trial, from punishment for any Murders which they should commit on the Inhabitants of these States:—For cutting off our Trade with all parts of the world:—For imposing Taxes on us without our Consent:—For depriving us in many cases, of the benefits of Trial by Jury:—For transporting us beyond Seas to be tried for pretended offences:—For abolishing the free System of English Laws in a neighbouring Province, establishing therein an Arbitrary government, and enlarging its Boundaries so as to render it at once an example and fit instrument for introducing the same absolute rule into these Colonies:—For taking away our Charters, abolishing our most valuable Laws, and altering fundamentally the Forms of our Governments:—For suspending our own Legislatures, and declaring themselves invested with power to legislate for us in all cases whatsoever.—He has abdicated Government here, by declaring us out of his Protection and waging War against us.—He has plundered our seas, ravaged our Coasts, burnt our towns, and destroyed the lives of our people.—He is at this time transporting large armies of foreign mercenaries to compleat the works of death, desolation and tyranny, already begun with circumstances of Cruelty & perfidy scarcely paralleled in the most barbarous ages, and totally unworthy the Head of a civilized nation.—He has constrained our fellow Citizens taken Captive on the high Seas to bear Arms against their Country, to become the executioners of their friends and Brethren, or to fall themselves by their Hands.—He has excited domestic insurrections amongst us, and has endeavoured to bring on the inhabitants of our frontiers, the merciless Indian Savages, whose known rule of warfare, is an undistinguished destruction of all ages, sexes and conditions. In every stage of these Oppressions We have Petitioned for Redress in the most humble terms: Our repeated Petitions have been answered only by repeated injury. A Prince, whose character is thus marked by every act which may define a Tyrant, is unfit to be the ruler of a free people. Nor have We been wanting in attentions to our British brethren. We have warned them from time to time of attempts by their legislature to extend an unwarrantable jurisdiction over us. We have reminded them of the circumstances of our emigration and settlement here. We have appealed to their native justice and magnanimity, and we have conjured them by the ties of our common kindred to disavow these usurpations, which, would inevitably interrupt our connections and correspondence. They too have been deaf to the voice of justice and of consanguinity. We must, therefore, acquiesce in the necessity, which denounces our Separation, and hold them, as we hold the rest of mankind, Enemies in War, in Peace Friends.—

We, Therefore, the Representatives of the United States of America, in General Congress, Assembled, appealing to the Supreme Judge of the world for the rectitude of our intentions, do, in the Name, and by Authority of the good People of these Colonies, solemnly publish and declare, That these United Colonies are, and of Right ought to be Free and Independent States; that they are Absolved from all Allegiance to the British Crown, and that all political connection between them and the State of Great Britain, is and ought to be totally dissolved; and that as Free and Independent States, they have full Power to levy War, conclude Peace, contract Alliances, establish Commerce, and to do all other Acts and Things which Independent States may of right do.—And for the support of this Declaration, with a firm reliance on the protection of Divine Providence, we mutually pledge to each other our Lives, our Fortunes and our sacred Honor.

JOHN HANCOCK.

New Hampshire

JOSIAH BARTLETT,
WM. WHIPPLE,
MATTHEW THORNTON.

Massachusetts Bay

SAML. ADAMS,
JOHN ADAMS,
ROBT. TREAT PAINE,
ELBRIDGE GERRY.

Rhode Island

STEP. HOPKINS,
WILLIAM ELLERY.

Connecticut

ROGER SHERMAN,
SAM'EL HUNTINGTON,
WM. WILLIAMS,
OLIVER WOLCOTT.

New York

WM. FLOYD,
PHIN. LIVINGSTON,
FRANS. LEWIS,
LEWIS MORRIS.

New Jersey

RICHD. STOCKTON,
JNO. WITHERSPOON,
FRAS. HOPKINSON,
JOHN HART,
ABRA. CLARK.

Pennsylvania

ROBT. MORRIS,
BENJAMIN RUSH,
BENJA. FRANKLIN,
JOHN MORTON,
GEO. CLYMER,
JAS. SMITH,
GEO. TAYLOR,
JAMES WILSON,
GEO. ROSS.

Delaware

CAESAR RODNEY,
GEO. READ,
THO. M'KEAN.

Maryland

SAMUEL CHASE,
WM. PACA,
THOS. STONE,
CHARLES CARROLL
of Carrollton.

Virginia

GEORGE WYTHE,
RICHARD HENRY LEE,
TH. JEFFERSON,
BENJA. HARRISON,
THS. NELSON, JR.,
FRANCIS LIGHTFOOT
LEE,
CARTER BRAXTON.

North Carolina

WM. HOOPER,
JOSEPH HEWES,
JOHN PENN.

South Carolina
EDWARD RUTLEDGE,
THOS. HEYWARD, JUNR.,
THOS. LYNCH, JUNR.,
ARTHUR MIDDLETON.

Georgia
BUTTON GWINNETT,
LYMAN HALL,
GEO. WALTON.

NOTES

NOTE.—Mr. Ferdinand Jefferson, Keeper of the Rolls in the Department of State, at Washington, says: "The names of the signers are spelt above as in the facsimile of the original, but the punctuation of them is not always the same; neither do the names of the States appear in the facsimile of the original. The names of the signers of each State are grouped together in the facsimile of the original, except the name of Matthew Thornton, which follows that of Oliver Wolcott."—*Revised Statutes of the United States, 2d edition, 1878, p. 6.*

[1] Reprinted from the facsimile of the engrossed copy of the original manuscript in the Library of Congress.

The Constitution of the United States[1]

We The People of the United States, in Order to form a more perfect Union, establish Justice, insure domestic Tranquility, provide for the common defence, promote the general Welfare, and secure the Blessings of Liberty to ourselves and our Posterity, do ordain and establish this Constitution for the United States of America.

ARTICLE. I.

Section. 1.

All legislative Powers herein granted shall be vested in a Congress of the United States, which shall consist of a Senate and House of Representatives.

Section. 2.

The House of Representatives shall be composed of Members chosen every second Year by the People of the several States, and the Electors in each State shall have the Qualifications requisite for Electors of the most numerous Branch of the State Legislature.

No person shall be a Representative who shall not have attained to the Age of twenty five years and been seven years a Citizen of the United States, and who shall not, when elected, be an Inhabitant of that State in which he shall be chosen.

Representatives and direct Taxes shall be apportioned among the several States which may be included within this Union, according to their respective Numbers, which shall be determined by adding to the whole Number of free Persons including those bound to Service for a Term of Years, and excluding Indians not taxed, three fifths of all other Persons. The actual Enumeration shall be made within three Years after the first Meeting of the Congress of the United States, and within every subsequent Term of ten Years, in such Manner as they shall by Law direct. The Number of Representatives shall not exceed one for every thirty Thousand, but each State shall have at Least one Representative; and until such enumeration shall be made, the State of New Hampshire shall be entitled to chuse three, Massachusetts eight, Rhode-Island and Providence Plantations one, Connecticut five, New-York six, New Jersey four, Pennsylvania eight, Delaware one, Maryland six, Virginia ten, North Carolina five, South Carolina five, and Georgia three.

When vacancies happen in the Representation from any State, the Executive Authority thereof shall issue Writs of Election to fill such Vacancies.

The House of Representatives shall chuse their Speaker and other Officers; and shall have the sole Power of Impeachment.

Section. 3.

The Senate of the United States shall be composed of two Senators from each State, chosen by the Legislature thereof, for six Years; and each Senator shall have one Vote.

Immediately after they shall be assembled in Consequence of the first Election, they shall be divided as equally as may be into three Classes. The Seats of the Senators of the first Class shall be vacated at the Expiration of the second Year, of the second Class at the Expiration of the fourth Year, and of the third Class at the Expiration of the sixth Year, so that one third may be chosen every second Year; and if Vacancies happen by Resignation, or otherwise, during the Recess of the Legislature of any State, the Executive thereof may make temporary Appointments until the next Meeting of the Legislature, which shall then fill such Vacancies.

No Person shall be a Senator who shall not have attained to the Age of thirty Years, and been nine Years a Citizen of the United States, and who shall not, when elected, be an Inhabitant of that State for which he shall be chosen.

The Vice President of the United States shall be President of the Senate, but shall have no Vote, unless they be equally divided.

The Senate shall chuse their other Officers, and also a President pro tempore, in the Absence of the Vice President, or when he shall exercise the Office of President of the United States.

The Senate shall have the sole Power to try all Impeachments. When sitting for that Purpose, they shall be on Oath or Affirmation. When the President of the United States is tried, the Chief Justice shall preside: And no Person shall be convicted without the Concurrence of two thirds of the Members present.

Judgment in Cases of Impeachment shall not extend further than to removal from Office, and disqualification to hold and enjoy any Office of honor, Trust or Profit under the United States: but the Party convicted shall nevertheless be liable and subject to Indictment, Trial, Judgment and Punishment, according to Law.

Section. 4.

The Times, Places and Manner of holding Elections for Senators and Representatives, shall be prescribed in each State by the Legislature thereof; but the Congress may at any time by Law make or alter such Regulations, except as to the Places of chusing Senators.

The Congress shall assemble at least once in every Year, and such Meeting shall be on the first Monday in December, unless they shall by Law appoint a different Day.

Section. 5.

Each House shall be the Judge of the Elections, Returns and Qualifications of its own Members, and a Majority of each shall constitute a Quorum to do Business; but a smaller Number may adjourn from day to day, and may be authorized to compel the Attendance of absent Members, in such Manner, and under such Penalties as each House may provide.

Each House may determine the Rules of its Proceedings, punish its Members for disorderly Behaviour, and, with the Concurrence of two thirds, expel a Member.

Each House shall keep a Journal of its Proceedings, and from time to time publish the same, excepting such Parts as may in their Judgment require Secrecy; and the Yeas and Nays of the Members of either House on any question shall, at the Desire of one fifth of those Present, be entered on the Journal.

Neither House, during the Session of Congress, shall, without the Consent of the other, adjourn for more than three days, nor to any other Place than that in which the two Houses shall be sitting.

Section. 6.

The Senators and Representatives shall receive a Compensation for their Services, to be ascertained by Law, and paid out of the Treasury of the United States. They shall in all Cases, except Treason, Felony and Breach of the Peace, be privileged from Arrest during their Attendance at the Session of their respective Houses, and in going to and returning from the same; and for any Speech or Debate in either House, they shall not be questioned in any other Place.

No Senator or Representative shall, during the Time for which he was elected, be appointed to any civil Office under the Authority of the United States, which shall have been created, or the Emoluments whereof shall have been encreased during such time; and no Person holding any Office under the United States, shall be a Member of either House during his Continuance in Office.

Section. 7.

All bills for raising Revenue shall originate in the House of Representatives; but the Senate may propose or concur with Amendments as on other Bills.

Every Bill which shall have passed the House of Representatives and the Senate, shall, before it become a Law, be presented to the

President of the United States; If he approves he shall sign it, but if not he shall return it, with his Objections to that House in which it shall have originated, who shall enter the Objections at large on their Journal, and proceed to reconsider it. If after such Reconsideration two thirds of that House shall agree to pass the Bill, it shall be sent, together with the Objections, to the other House, by which it shall likewise be reconsidered, and if approved by two thirds of that House, it shall become a Law. But in all such Cases the Votes of both Houses shall be determined by yeas and Nays, and the Names of the Persons voting for and against the Bill shall be entered on the Journal of each House respectively. If any Bill shall not be returned by the President within ten days (Sundays excepted) after it shall have been presented to him, the Same shall be a Law, in like Manner as if he had signed it, unless the Congress by their Adjournment prevent its Return in which Case it shall not be a Law.

Every Order, Resolution, or Vote to which the Concurrence of the Senate and House of Representatives may be necessary (except on a question of Adjournment) shall be presented to the President of the United States; and before the Same shall take Effect, shall be approved by him, or being disapproved by him, shall be repassed by two thirds of the Senate and House of Representatives, according to the Rules and Limitations prescribed in the Case of a Bill.

Section. 8.

The Congress shall have Power To lay and collect Taxes, Duties, Imposts and Excises, to pay the Debts and provide for the common Defence and general Welfare of the United States; but all Duties, Imposts and Excises shall be uniform throughout the United States;

To borrow Money on the credit of the United States;

To regulate Commerce with foreign Nations, and among the several States, and with the Indian Tribes;

To establish an uniform Rule of Naturalization, and uniform Laws on the subject of Bankruptcies throughout the United States;

To coin Money, regulate the Value thereof, and of foreign Coin, and fix the Standard of Weights and Measures;

To provide for the Punishment of counterfeiting the Securities and current Coin of the United States;

To establish Post Offices and post Roads;

To promote the Progress of Science and useful Arts, by securing for limited Times to Authors and Inventors the exclusive Right to their respective Writings and Discoveries;

To constitute Tribunals inferior to the supreme Court;

To define and punish Piracies and Felonies committed on the high Seas, and Offenses against the Law of Nations;

To declare War, grant Letters of Marque and Reprisal, and make Rules concerning Captures on Land and Water;

To raise and support Armies, but no Appropriation of Money to that Use shall be for a longer Term than two Years;

To provide and maintain a Navy;

To make Rules for the Government and Regulation of the land and naval Forces;

To provide for calling forth the Militia to execute the Laws of the Union, suppress Insurrections and repel Invasions;

To provide for organizing, arming, and disciplining, the Militia, and for governing such Part of them as may be employed in the Service of the United States, reserving to the States respectively, the Appointment of the Officers, and the Authority of training the Militia according to the discipline prescribed by Congress;

To exercise exclusive Legislation in all Cases whatsoever, over such District (not exceeding ten Miles square) as may, by Cession of particular States, and the Acceptance of Congress, become the Seat of the Government of the United States, and to exercise like

Authority over all Places purchased by the Consent of the Legislature of the State in which the Same shall be, for the Erection of Forts, Magazines, Arsenals, dock-Yards, and other needful Buildings;—And

To make all Laws which shall be necessary and proper for carrying into Execution the foregoing Powers, and all other Powers vested by this Constitution in the Government of the United States, or in any Department or Office thereof.

Section. 9.

The Migration or Importation of such Persons as any of the States now existing shall think proper to admit, shall not be prohibited by the Congress prior to the Year one thousand eight hundred and eight, but a Tax or duty may be imposed on such Importation, not exceeding ten dollars for each Person.

The Privilege of the Writ of Habeas Corpus shall not be suspended, unless when in Cases of Rebellion or Invasion the public Safety may require it.

No Bill of Attainder or ex post facto Law shall be passed.

No Capitation, or other direct, Tax shall be laid, unless in Proportion to the Census or Enumeration herein before directed to be taken.

No Tax or Duty shall be laid on Articles exported from any State.

No Preference shall be given by any Regulation of Commerce or Revenue to the Ports of one State over those of another: nor shall Vessels bound to, or from, one State, be obliged to enter, clear, or pay Duties in another.

No Money shall be drawn from the Treasury, but in Consequence of Appropriations made by Law; and a regular Statement and Account of the Receipts and Expenditures of all public Money shall be published from time to time.

No Title of Nobility shall be granted by the United States: And no Person holding any Office of Profit or Trust under them, shall, without the Consent of the Congress, accept of any present, Emolument, Office, or Title, of any kind whatever, from any King, Prince, or foreign State.

Section. 10.

No State shall enter into any Treaty, Alliance, or Confederation; grant Letters of Marque and Reprisal; coin Money; emit Bills of Credit; make any Thing but gold and silver Coin a Tender in Payment of Debts; pass any Bill of Attainder, ex post facto Law, or Law imparing the Obligation of Contracts, or grant any Title of Nobility.

No State shall, without the Consent of the Congress, lay any Imposts or Duties on Imports or Exports, except what may be absolutely necessary for executing it's inspection Laws: and the net Produce of all Duties and Imposts, laid by any State on Imports or Exports, shall be for the Use of the Treasury of the United States; and all such Laws shall be subject to the Revision and Controul of the Congress.

No State shall, without the Consent of Congress, lay any Duty of Tonnage, keep Troops, or Ships of War in time of Peace, enter into any Agreement or Compact with another State, or with a foreign Power, or engage in War, unless actually invaded, or in such imminent Danger as will not admit of delay.

ARTICLE. II.

Section. 1.

The executive Power shall be vested in a President of the United States of America. He shall hold his Office during the Term of four Years, and, together with the Vice President, chosen for the same Term, be elected as follows

Each State shall appoint, in such Manner as the Legislature thereof may direct, a Number of Electors, equal to the whole Number of

Senators and Representatives to which the State may be entitled in the Congress: but no Senator or Representative, or Person holding an Office of Trust or Profit under the United States, shall be appointed an Elector.

The Electors shall meet in their respective States, and vote by Ballot for two Persons, of whom one at least shall not be an Inhabitant of the same State with themselves. And they shall make a List of all the Persons voted for, and of the Number of Votes for each; which List they shall sign and certify, and transmit sealed to the Seat of the Government of the United States, directed to the President of the Senate. The President of the Senate shall, in the Presence of the Senate and House of Representatives, open all the Certificates, and the Votes shall then be counted. The Person having the greatest Number of Votes shall be the President, if such Number be a Majority of the whole Number of Electors appointed; and if there be more than one who have such Majority, and have an equal Number of Votes, then the House of Representatives shall immediately chuse by Ballot one of them for President; and if no Person have a Majority, then from the five highest on the List the said House shall in like Manner chuse the President. But in chusing the President, the Votes shall be taken by States, the Representation from each State having one Vote; A quorum for this Purpose shall consist of a Member or Members from two thirds of the States, and a Majority of all the States shall be necessary to a Choice. In every Case, after the Choice of the President, the Person having the greatest Number of Votes of the Electors shall be the Vice President. But if there should remain two or more who have equal Votes, the Senate shall chuse from them by Ballot the Vice President.

The Congress may determine the Time of chusing the Electors, and the Day on which they shall give their Votes; which Day shall be the same throughout the United States.

No Person except a natural born Citizen, or a Citizen of the United States, at the time of the Adoption of this Constitution, shall be eligible to the Office of President; neither shall any Person be eligible to that Office who shall not have attained to the Age of thirty five Years, and been fourteen Years a Resident within the United States.

In Case of the Removal of the President from Office, or of his Death, Resignation, or Inability to discharge the Powers and Duties of the said Office, the Same shall devolve on the Vice President, and the Congress may by Law provide for the Case of Removal, Death, Resignation or Inability, both of the President and Vice President, declaring what Officer shall then act as President, and such Officer shall act accordingly, until the Disability be removed, or a President shall be elected.

The President shall, at stated Times, receive for his Services, a Compensation, which shall neither be encreased nor diminished during the Period for which he shall have been elected, and he shall not receive within that Period any other Emolument from the United States, or any of them.

Before he enter on the Execution of his Office, he shall take the following Oath or Affirmation:—"I do solemnly swear (or affirm) that I will faithfully execute the Office of President of the United States, and will to the best of my Ability, preserve, protect and defend the Constitution of the United States."

Section. 2.

The President shall be Commander in Chief of the Army and Navy of the United States, and of the Militia of the several States, when called into the actual Service of the United States; he may require the Opinion, in writing, of the principal Officer in each of the executive Departments, upon any Subject relating to the Duties of their respective Offices, and he shall have Power to grant Reprieves and Pardons for Offences against the United States, except in Cases of Impeachment.

He shall have Power, by and with the Advice and Consent of the Senate, to make Treaties, provided two thirds of the Senators present concur; and he shall nominate, and by and with the Advice and Consent of the Senate, shall appoint Ambassadors, other public Ministers and Consuls, Judges of the supreme Court, and all other Officers of the United States, whose Appointments are not herein otherwise provided for, and which shall be established by Law: but the Congress may by Law vest the Appointment of such inferior Officers, as they think proper, in the President alone, in the Courts of Law, or in the Heads of Departments.

The President shall have Power to fill up all Vacancies that may happen during the Recess of the Senate, by granting Commissions which shall expire at the End of their next Session.

Section. 3.

He shall from time to time give to the Congress Information of the State of the Union, and recommend to their Consideration such Measures as he shall judge necessary and expedient; he may, on extraordinary Occasions, convene both Houses, or either of them, and in Case of Disagreement between them, with Respect to the Time of Adjournment, he may adjourn them to such Time as he shall think proper; he shall receive Ambassadors and other public Ministers; he shall take Care that the Laws be faithfully executed, and shall Commission all the Officers of the United States.

Section. 4.

The President, Vice President and all civil Officers of the United States, shall be removed from Office on Impeachment for, and Conviction of, Treason, Bribery, or other high Crimes and Misdemeanors.

ARTICLE. III.

Section. 1.

The judicial Power of the United States, shall be vested in one supreme Court, and in such inferior Courts as the Congress may from time to time ordain and establish. The Judges, both of the supreme and inferior Courts, shall hold their Offices during good Behaviour, and shall, at stated Times, receive for their Services, a

Compensation, which shall not be diminished during their Continuance in Office.

Section. 2.

The judicial Power shall extend to all Cases, in Law and Equity, arising under this Constitution, the Laws of the United States, and Treaties made, or which shall be made, under their Authority;—to all Cases affecting Ambassadors, other public Ministers and Consuls;—to all Cases of admiralty and maritime Jurisdiction;—to Controversies to which the United States shall be a Party;—to Controversies between two or more States;—between a State and Citizens of another State;—between Citizens of different States,—between Ciizens of the same State claiming Lands under Grants of different States, and between a State, or the Citizens thereof, and foreign States, Citizens or Subjects.

In all Cases affecting Ambassadors, other public Ministers and Consuls, and those in which a State shall be Party, the supreme Court shall have original Jurisdiction. In all the other Cases before mentioned, the supreme Court shall have appellate Jurisdiction, both as to Law and Fact, with such Exceptions, and under such Regulations as the Congress shall make.

The Trial of all Crimes, except in Cases of Impeachment, shall be by Jury; and such Trial shall be held in the State where the said Crimes shall have been committed; but when not committed within any State, the Trial shall be at such Place or Places as the Congress may by Law have directed.

Section. 3.

Treason against the United States, shall consist only in levying War against them, or in adhering to their Enemies, giving them Aid and Comfort. No Person shall be convicted of Treason unless on the Testimony of two Witnesses to the same overt Act, or on Confession in open Court.

The Congress shall have Power to declare the Punishment of Treason, but no Attainder of Treason shall work Corruption of Blood, or Forfeiture except during the Life of the Person attainted.

ARTICLE. IV.

Section. 1.

Full Faith and Credit shall be given in each State to the public Acts, Records, and judicial Proceedings of every other State. And the Congress may by general Laws prescribe the Manner in which such Acts, Records and Proceedings shall be proved, and the Effect thereof.

The Citizens of each State shall be entitled to all Privileges and Immunities of Citizens in the several States.

A Person charged by any State with Treason, Felony, or other Crime, who shall flee from Justice, and be found in another State, shall on Demand of the executive Authority of the State from which he fled, be delivered up, to be removed to the State having Jurisdiction of the Crime.

No Person held to Service or Labour in one State, under the Laws thereof, escaping into another, shall, in Consequence of any Law or Regulation therein, be discharged from such Service or Labour, but shall be delivered up on Claim of the Party to whom such Service or Labour may be due.

Section. 3.

New States may be admitted by the Congress into this Union; but no new State shall be formed or erected within the Jurisdiction of any other State; nor any State be formed by the Junction of two or more States, or Parts of States, without the Consent of the Legislatures of the States concerned as well as of the Congress.

The Congress shall have Power to dispose of and make all needful Rules and Regulations respecting the Territory or other Property belonging to the United States; and nothing in this Constitution shall be so construed as to Prejudice any Claims of the United States, or of any particular State.

Section. 4.

The United States shall guarantee to every State in this Union a Republican Form of Government, and shall protect each of them against Invasion; and on Application of the Legislature, or of the Executive (when the Legislature cannot be convened) against domestic Violence.

ARTICLE. V.

The Congress, whenever two thirds of both Houses shall deem it necessary, shall propose Amendments to this Constitution, or, on the Application of the Legislatures of two thirds of the several states, shall call a Convention for proposing Amendments, which, in either Case, shall be valid to all Intents and Purposes, as Part of this Constitution, when ratified by the Legislatures of three fourths of the several States, or by Conventions in three fourths thereof, as the one or the other Mode of Ratification may be proposed by the Congress; Provided that no Amendment which may be made prior to the Year One thousand eight hundred and eight shall in any Manner affect the first and fourth Clauses in the Ninth Section of the first Article; and that no State, without its Consent, shall be deprived of it's equal Suffrage in the Senate.

ARTICLE. VI.

All Debts contracted and Engagements entered into, before the Adoption of this Constitution, shall be as valid against the United States under this Constitution, as under the Confederation.

This Constitution, and the Laws of the United States which shall be made in Pursuance thereof; and all Treaties made, or which shall be made, under the Authority of the United States, shall be the supreme Law of the Land; and the Judges in every State shall be bound thereby, any Thing in the Constitution or Laws of any State to the Contrary notwithstanding.

The Senators and Representatives before mentioned, and the Members of the several State Legislatures, and all executive and judicial Officers, both of the United States and of the several States, shall be bound by Oath or Affirmation, to support this Constitution; but no religious Test shall ever be required as a Qualification to any Office or public Trust under the United States.

ARTICLE. VII.

The Ratification of the Conventions of nine States, shall be sufficient for the Establishment of this Constitution between the States so ratifying the Same.

The Word, "the," being interlined between the seventh and eighth Lines of the first Page, The Word "Thirty" being partly written on an Erazure in the fifteenth Line of the first Page, The Words "is tried" being interlined between the thirty second and thirty third Lines of the first Page and the Word "the" being interlined between the forty third and forty fourth Lines of the second Page [Done] in Convention by the unanimous Consent of the States present the Seventeenth Day of September in the Year of our Lord one thousand seven hundred and Eighty seven and of The Independance of the United States of America the Twelfth In witness whereof We have hereunto subscribed our Names,

G⁰ WASHINGTON—Presidᵗ
and deputy from Virginia

Attest WILLIAM JACKSON
Secretary

New Hampshire
John Langdon
Nicholas Gilman

Massachusetts
Nathaniel Gorham
Rufus King

Connecticut
  Wm Saml Johnson
  Roger Sherman

New York
  Alexander Hamilton

New Jersey
  Wil: Livingston
  David Brearley
  Wm Paterson
  Jona: Dayton

Pennsylvania
  B Franklin
  Thomas Mifflin
  Robt Morris
  Geo. Clymer
  Thos Fitzsimons
  Jared Ingersoll
  James Wilson
  Gouv Morris

Delaware
  Geo: Read
  Gunning Bedford jun
  John Dickinson
  Richard Basset
  Jaco: Broom

Maryland
  James McHenry
  Dan of St Thos Jenifer
  Danl Carroll

Virginia
  John Blair—
  James Madison Jr.

North Carolina
  Wm Blount
  Richd Dobbs Spaight
  Hu Williamson

South Carolina
  J. Rutledge
  Charles Cotesworth Pinckney
  Charles Pinckney
  Pierce Butler

Georgia
  William Few
  Abr Baldwin

AMENDMENTS TO THE UNITED STATES CONSTITUTION

Amendment I

[Ratification of the first ten amendments was completed December 15, 1791]

Congress shall make no law respecting an establishment of religion, or prohibiting the free exercise thereof; or abridging the freedom of speech, or of the press; or the right of the people peaceably to assemble, and to petition the Government for a redress of grievances.

Amendment II

A well regulated Militia, being necessary to the security of a free State, the right of the people to keep and bear Arms, shall not be infringed.

Amendment III

No Soldier shall, in time of peace be quartered in any house, without the consent of the Owner, nor in time of war, but in a manner to be prescribed by law.

Amendment IV

The right of the people to be secure in their persons, houses, papers, and effects, against unreasonable searches and seizures, shall not be violated, and no Warrants shall issue, but upon probable cause, supported by Oath or affirmation, and particularly describing the place to be searched, and the persons or things to be seized.

Amendment V

No person shall be held to answer for a capital, or otherwise infamous crime, unless on a presentment or indictment of a Grand Jury, except in cases arising in the land or naval forces, or in the Militia, when in actual service in time of War or public danger; nor shall any person be subject for the same offence to be twice put in jeopardy of life or limb; nor shall be compelled in any criminal case to be a witness against himself, nor be deprived of life, liberty, or property, without due process of law; nor shall private property be taken for public use, without just compensation.

Amendment VI

In all criminal prosecutions, the accused shall enjoy the right to a speedy and public trial, by an impartial jury of the State and district wherein the crime shall have been committed, which district shall have been previously ascertained by law, and to be informed of the nature and cause of the accusation; to be confronted with the witness against him; to have compulsory process for obtaining witness in his favor, and to have the Assistance of Counsel for his defence.

Amendment VII

In Suits at common law, where the value in controversy shall exceed twenty dollars, the right of trial by jury shall be preserved, and no fact tried by a jury, shall be otherwise re-examined in any Court of the United States, than according to the rules of the common law.

Amendment VIII

Excessive bail shall not be required, nor excessive fines imposed, nor cruel and unusual punishments inflicted.

Amendment IX

The enumeration in the Constitution, of certain rights, shall not be construed to deny or disparage others retained by the people.

Amendment X

The powers not delegated to the United States by the Constitution, nor prohibited by it to the States, are reserved to the States respectively, or to the people.

Amendment XI *[January 8, 1798]*

The Judicial power of the United States shall not be construed to extend to any suit in law or equity, commenced or prosecuted against one of the United States by Citizens of another State, or by Citizens or Subjects of any Foreign State.

Amendment XII *[September 25, 1804]*

The Electors shall meet in their respective states and vote by ballot for President and Vice-President, one of whom, at least, shall not be an inhabitant of the same state with themselves; they shall name in their ballots the person voted for as President, and in distinct ballots the person voted for as Vice-President, and they shall make distinct lists of all persons voted for as President, and of all persons voted for as Vice-President, and of the number of votes for each, which lists they shall sign and certify, and transmit sealed to the seat of the government of the United States, directed to the President of the Senate—The President of the Senate shall, in the presence of Senate and House of Representatives, open all the certificates and the votes shall then be counted;—The person having the greatest number of votes for President, shall be the President, if such number be a majority of the whole number of Electors appointed; and if no person have such a majority, then from the persons having the highest numbers not exceeding three on the list of those voted for as President, the House of Representatives shall choose immediately, by ballot, the President. But in choosing the President, the votes shall be taken by states, the representation from each state having one vote; a quorum for this purpose shall consist of a member or members from two-thirds of the states, and a majority of all the states shall be necessary to a choice. And if the House of Representatives shall not choose a President whenever the right of choice shall devolve upon them, before the fourth day of March next following, then the Vice-President shall act as President, as in the case of the death or other constitutional disability of the President.—The person having the greatest number of votes as Vice-President, shall be the Vice-President, if such number be a majority of the whole number of Electors appointed, and if no person have a majority, then from the two highest numbers on the list, the Senate shall choose the Vice-President; a quorum for the purpose shall consist of two-thirds of the whole number of Senators, and a majority of the whole number shall be necessary to a choice. But no person constitutionally ineligible to the office of President shall be eligible to that of Vice-President of the United States.

Amendment XIII *[December 18, 1865]*

Section 1. Neither slavery nor involuntary servitude, except as a punishment for crime whereof the party shall have been duly convicted, shall exist within the United States, or any place subject to their jurisdiction.

Section 2. Congress shall have power to enforce this article by appropriate legislation.

Amendment XIV *[July 28, 1868]*

Section 1. All persons born or naturalized in the United States, and subject to the jurisdiction thereof, are citizens of the United States and of the State wherein they reside. No State shall make or enforce any law which shall abridge the privileges or immunities of citizens of the United States; nor shall any state deprive any person of life, liberty, or property, without due process of law; nor deny to any person within its jurisdiction the equal protection of the laws.

Section 2. Representatives shall be apportioned among the several States according to their respective numbers, counting the whole number of persons in each State, excluding Indians not taxed. But when the right to vote at any election for the choice of electors for President and Vice President of the United States, Representatives in Congress, the Executive and Judicial officers of a State, or the members of the Legislature thereof, is denied to any of the male inhabitants of such State, being twenty-one years of age, and citizens of the United States, or in any way abridged, except for participation in rebellion, or other crime, the basis of representation therein shall be reduced in the proportion which the number of such male citizens shall bear to the whole number of male citizens twenty-one years of age in such State.

Section 3. No person shall be a Senator or Representative in Congress, or elector of President and Vice President, or hold any office, civil or military, under the United States, or under any State, who, having previously taken an oath, as a member of Congress, or as an officer of the United States, or as a member of any State legislature, or as an executive or judicial officer of any State, to support the Constitution of the United States, shall have engaged in insurrection or rebellion against the same, or given aid or comfort to the enemies thereof. But Congress may by a vote of two-thirds of each House, remove such disability.

Section 4. The validity of the public debt of the United States, authorized by law, including debts incurred for payment of pensions and bounties for services in suppressing insurrection or rebellion, shall not be questioned. But neither the United States nor any State shall assume or pay any debt or obligation incurred in aid of insurrection or rebellion against the United States, or any claim for the loss or emancipation of any slave; but all such debts, obligations and claims shall be held illegal and void.

Section 5. The Congress shall have power to enforce, by appropriate legislation, the provisions of this article.

Amendment XV *[March 30, 1870]*

Section 1. The right of citizens of the United States to vote shall not be denied or abridged by the United States or by any State on account of race, color, or previous condition of servitude.

Section 2. The Congress shall have power to enforce this article by appropriate legislation.

Amendment XVI *[February 25, 1913]*

The Congress shall have power to lay and collect taxes on incomes, from whatever source derived, without apportionment among the several States, and without regard to any census or enumeration.

Amendment XVII *[May 31, 1913]*

The Senate of the United States shall be composed of two Senators from each State, elected by the people thereof, for six years; and each Senator shall have one vote. The electors in each State shall have the qualifications requisite for electors of the most numerous branch of the State legislatures.

When vacancies happen in the representation of any State in the Senate, the executive authority of such State shall issue writs of election to fill such vacancies: *Provided,* That the legislature of any State may empower the executive thereof to make temporary appointments until the people fill the vacancies by election as the legislature may direct.

This amendment shall not be so construed as to affect the election or term of any Senator chosen before it becomes valid as part of the Constitution.

Amendment XVIII *[January 29, 1919]*

Section 1. After one year from the ratification of this article the manufacture, sale, or transportation of intoxicating liquors within, the importation thereof into, or the exportation thereof from the United States and all territory subject to the jurisdiction thereof for beverage purposes is hereby prohibited.

Section 2. The Congress and the several States shall have concurrent power to enforce this article by appropriate legislation.

Section 3. This article shall be inoperative unless it shall have been ratified as an amendment to the Constitution by the legislatures of the several States, as provided in the Constitution, within seven years from the date of the submission hereof to the States by the Congress.

Amendment XIX *[August 26, 1920]*

The right of citizens of the United States to vote shall not be denied or abridged by the United States or by any State on account of sex.

Congress shall have power to enforce this article by appropriate legislation.

Amendment XX *[February 6, 1933]*

Section 1. The terms of the President and Vice President shall end at noon on the 20th day of January, and the terms of Senators and Representatives at noon on the 3d day of January, of the years in which such terms would have ended if this article had not been ratified; and the terms of their successors shall then begin.

Section 2. The Congress shall assemble at least once in every year, and such meeting shall begin at noon on the 3d day of January, unless they shall by law appoint a different day.

Section 3. If at the time fixed for the beginning of the term of the President, the President elect shall have died, the Vice President elect shall become President. If a President shall not have been chosen before the time fixed for the beginning of his term, or if the President elect shall have failed to qualify, then the Vice President elect shall act as President until a President shall have qualified; and the Congress may by law provide for the case wherein neither a President elect nor a Vice President elect shall have qualified, declaring who shall then act as President, or the manner in which one who is to act shall be selected, and such person shall act accordingly until a President or Vice President shall have qualified.

Section 4. The Congress may by law provide for the case of the death of any of the persons from whom the House of Representatives may choose a President whenever the right of choice shall have devolved upon them, and for the case of the death of any of the persons from whom the Senate may choose a Vice President whenever the right of choice shall have devolved upon them.

Section 5. Sections 1 and 2 shall take effect on the 15th day of October following the ratification of this article.

Section 6. This article shall be inoperative unless it shall have been ratified as an amendment to the Constitution by the legislatures of three-fourths of the several States within seven years from the date of its submission.

Amendment XXI *[December 5, 1933]*

Section 1. The eighteenth article of amendment to the Constitution of the United States is hereby repealed.

Section 2. The transportation or importation into any State, Territory, or possession of the United States for delivery or use therein of intoxicating liquors, in violation of the laws thereof, is hereby prohibited.

Section 3. This article shall be inoperative unless it shall have been ratified as an amendment to the Constitution by conventions in the several States, as provided in the Constitution, within seven years from the date of the submission hereof to the States by the Congress.

Amendment XXII *[February 26, 1951]*

Section 1. No person shall be elected to the office of the President more than twice, and no person who has held the office of President, or acted as President, for more than two years of a term to which some other person was elected President shall be elected to the office of President more than once. But this Article shall not apply to any person holding the office of President when this Article was proposed by the Congress, and shall not prevent any person who may be holding the office of President, or acting as President, during the term within which this Article becomes operative from holding the office of President or acting as President during the remainder of such term.

Section 2. This article shall be inoperative unless it shall have been ratified as an amendment to the Constitution by the legislatures of three-fourths of the several States within seven years from the date of its submission of the States by the Congress.

Amendment XXIII *[March 29, 1961]*

Section 1. The District constituting the seat of Government of the United States shall appoint in such manner as the Congress may direct: A number of electors of President and Vice President equal to the whole number of Senators and Representatives in Congress to which the District would be entitled if it were a State, but in no event more than the least populous State; they shall be in addition to those appointed by the States, but they shall be considered, for the purposes of the election of President and Vice President, to be electors appointed by a State; and they shall meet in the District and perform such duties as provided by the twelfth article of amendment.

Section 2. The Congress shall have power to enforce this article by appropriate legislation.

Amendment XXIV *[January 23, 1964]*

Section 1. The right of citizens of the United States to vote in any primary or other election for President or Vice President, for electors for President or Vice President, or for Senator or Representative in Congress, shall not be denied or abridged by the United States or any State by reason of failure to pay any poll tax or other tax.

Section 2. The Congress shall have the power to enforce this article by appropriate legislation.

NOTE

[1] Reprinted from a literal copy of the engrossed Constitution as signed. The original is in four sheets, with an additional sheet containing the resolutions of transmittal. The note indented at the end is in the original precisely as reproduced here.